I AM TAMAR

THE SPIRITUAL WARFARE

of

Love and Relationships

BY CHARITY E. NORTHAN, MS, MA

TABLE OF CONTENTS

PREFACE

K ing David had a great number of sons by his wives and concubines. Amnon was the eldest son of King David. Among King David's other sons, was Absalom. The Bible names Tamar as Absalom's sister, which indicates they were born from the same mother. Tamar, along with being beautiful, was also a virgin. Ultimately, the eldest brother, Amnon, raped Tamar. Although it was indeed a tragedy, the abuse Tamar suffered neither began nor did it end with the rape. Very similar to many of our personal stories, Tamar's suffering was not restricted to the sexual abuse that characterized her rape. As the story goes, Tamar suffered abuse on multiple levels including emotional, physical, sexual, verbal, and spiritual. More lethal than the physical and sexual turmoil she suffered, was the emotional damage which left her spirit shattered and in despair. A path that started out so innocently for Tamar ended in tragedy. It is unknown what ever happened to Tamar except that she remained desolate in her brother Absalom's home.

Like Tamar, there are many of us, who have suffered from abuse and, up until this time, have remained desolate in our life. The purpose of this book is to help people identify and ultimately heal from emotional abuse. It is essential for us to understand the signs and symptoms of emotional abuse, the mentality of the abuser, and most importantly, the affects of emotional abuse on the spirit. We are Tamar, but we do not have to remain desolate. Thank God, we can heal, live, and bear fruit.

Introduction:

INTEGRATION OF COUNSELING AND SPIRITUALITY

T he counseling field has been around for several
centuries, even as far back as biblical times. In
times past, counselors were called advisors, elders, or
oracles. Counseling is one of the largest helping profes-
sions in today's society. Still, counselors carry various
titles including social worker, therapist, clinician, case
manager, etc. As well, there are many people serving
as counselors without professional titles. In actuality,
counselors come from all walks of life.

People from various social and economic statuses utilize counseling to address the issues of life. Counselors
do not solve problems; they merely provide skills to help
people cope with their past and current issues. They
also teach people skills to handle future concerns in a
way that will create and maintain interpersonal peace.
Overall, the field of counseling has been very successful.

Still, despite the proven success of counseling,
there is a large population that is reluctant to utilize

counseling due to either the cost, the negative stigma associated with mental health issues, or their idea that they would much rather consult a pastor or spiritual leader with their concerns. Many people of faith believe mental health issues are a result of some level of spiritual lacking or demonic warfare for which standard counseling cannot help. Many believe it is more beneficial to consult a pastor, have him anoint them with oil, and pray the prayer of faith over them than to see a regular counselor. That is, a growing number of parishioners prefer to make appointments with their pastors if they feel it necessary to talk to someone. More and more, clergy members are providing pastoral care sessions to assist parishioners with mental health issues.

Unfortunately, many religious leaders are not well equipped to address mental health issues because of a lack of education, preparation, training, and/or experience in the field. For example, a pastor may not know the specifics of a schizoaffective diagnosis and may suggest an exorcism rather than encourage the parishioner to, in addition to prayer, continue his prescribed medications and follow up with his psychiatrist.

There are many who agree that there is a need for a mixture of both counseling skills and spiritual advisement—Christian counseling. The dilemma in going to a Christian counselor for many believers, however, is that the average Christian counselor does not explore deep spiritual conviction as it relates to mental health. Too often, Christian counselors mention the Bible only in the broadest of aspects i.e., those that are applicable across all faiths and beliefs. The average Christian counselor does not go into depth about the function of evil spirits and demons, or generational curses in the manifestation of mental health issues. Consequently, there exists a large population who will not continue with a Christian counselor because their deep spiritual convictions are not addressed.

I discovered many years ago that God's purpose for my life is to integrate deep convictions of biblical truth into the field of counseling and vice versa. As a professional counselor, I do believe in the effectiveness of counseling to a certain extent. That is, we all need someone who will listen, help us process our issues, and teach us positive skills to move forward. As a believer, however, my conviction is that, even with the most effective counseling methods, we do not have the power or ability within our flesh to implement effective change into our daily life. It takes us walking in the Spirit and the power of the Holy Ghost to effectively heal and change our minds.

Beyond integrating counseling and Biblical conviction, I have a burden to minister to the world from an end time perspective. There is no greater purpose than to teach people about God's love and prepare the world for the end times. The purpose of this book is to address the topic of emotional abuse with biblical principles and deep spiritual conviction and, most important, to prepare the world for the second coming of Christ.

DEDICATION

In loving memory of Reginia Church Northan
August 1, 1956 – November 28, 2011

D uring the time my mother was sick and dying, I struggled to recover from a tumultuous marriage that eventually led to a divorce. Even basic self-esteem, self-confidence, and femininity were absent. In addition, the fact I was now a single mother left me in a state of shock. I fought to rid myself of depression and regain an identity that had long been lost. In addition to her own sickness, she cried and prayed for me. She had such high hopes for me and over the recent years, I had become someone completely different. My joy was gone; pain was all over my face. If only I had listened to my parents who were a man and woman of God.

In November of 2011, my mother finished her battle with cancer and went home to be with the Lord. Unfortunately, she never had a chance to see me recovering. Now that my healing has begun, I wish my mother were here to see me. My prayer and belief is that she is able to look down from heaven and see that God is turning it around for my good. I hope she can see how

God used my pain and suffering to give me a testimony. I had to go through it so that God would get the glory out of my life. I had to be processed for purpose. I did not regain my old identity, but I have obtained a new, much stronger identity in Christ. He has turned my mourning into dancing. All is not lost; God is getting the glory out of this.

FOREWORD

W hile there has been deep awareness in recent years regarding domestic abuse and violence against women, not much has been discussed on the elusive subject and devastating effects of emotional abuse against women. Even though emotional abuse does not leave physical scars, it is said to be the hardest type of abuse to understand and escape.

In *I Am Tamar: The Spiritual Warfare of Love and Relationships*, Charity Northan courageously delves into this sensitive topic with insight, wisdom, and clarity. She has powerfully combined her unique background in psychology, crisis counseling, and ministry to give us an in depth biblical analysis of emotional abuse from the viewpoint of both the victim and abuser.

This is a must-read for every woman who has suffered or is still suffering from emotional abuse in her life. You can recover and be made whole.

A big salute to Charity, who on a daily basis, remains on the front lines for those suffering from emotional abuse. As a professional counselor and ordained minister, Charity is like the Good Samaritan of old. She is bandaging the invisible wounds—pouring on the oil and wine of healing and hope to those that are hurting.

I, too, was once a Tamar, but I have emerged healed and strong. I pray that as you venture into this book, you will do the same.

Ann-Marie Brewer
Author
Fighting All Hell For Your Marriage, Your Man and Your Babies

EPIGRAPH

"For this cause I bow my knees unto the Father of our Lord Jesus Christ, of whom the whole family in heaven and earth is named, That he would grant you, according to the riches of his glory, to be strengthened with might by his Spirit in the inner man; That Christ may dwell in your hearts by faith; that ye, being rooted and grounded in love, May be able to comprehend with all saints what is the breadth, and length, and depth, and height; And to know the love of Christ, which passeth knowledge, that ye might be filled with all the fullness of God. Now unto him that is able to do exceeding abundantly above all that we ask or think, according to the power that worketh in us, unto him be glory in the church by Christ Jesus throughout all ages, world without end. Amen"
(Eph. 3:14-21, King James Version).

Chapter I

THE WAR ON TERRORISM AND THE SECOND COMING OF CHRIST

W e all can acknowledge the presence of tumultuous times. The once normal way of living has changed for the worse. Take for example, the 911 events in 2001. Many of us can recall what we were doing the morning of the attack. More recently was the Connecticut shooting in December of 2012. People all over the world were distraught and in disarray with the knowledge that someone would shoot and kill small, innocent children. Many children, those in Connecticut and around the world, continue to live in fear of attending school; they are terrorized with fear of someone attacking them, their classmates, or their family members. As well, many adults continue to carry feelings of anger, hurt, pain, panic, and fear. Our spirit remains unsettled long after the event is over. People who would normally be characterized as easy going and happy-go-lucky, are distracted with overwhelming feelings of suspicion and revenge.

As a nation, post-terrorist attack, we immediately start looking for someone to blame. We assign all of our resources to finding and tormenting the parties responsible. We hunt down, arrest, and judge anyone involved in carrying out such awful acts of terrorist. Psychiatrists, philosophers, researchers, historians, and the media do their best to make sense of why anyone would do such awful things. In response to terrorist attacks, various national organizations come in to repair the visible structural damages and address the immediate needs of the victims and hurting community i.e. medical care, clothing, food, temporary housing, counseling, burial, etc.. Politicians and celebrities hone in on the attention created by the disasters. Various religious organizations raise love offerings and publically stand in agreement for God to cover the victims. Months later, believers have stopped praying, the larger organizations are long gone, and victims are ill advised to 'get over it.' Unfortunately, the damage from terrorist attacks cannot be addressed all at once. For the victims, they are so overwhelmed with funeral arrangements and the media that they are not able to process all of what has happened to them. Very often, victims remain in shock. It is not until much later that signs of anxiety; anger, fear, and rage start to surface.

As believers, we must stop and look at the big picture. The real terrorist is Satan and these attacks come from him. Remember, Satan comes to kill, steal, and to destroy. Terrorist attacks are a device from Satan to destroy the spirit of humankind. Satan has always been and will always be after the souls of the world. His number one goal is to acquire as many souls as possible before he is eternally damned to the lake of fire, and he will do anything he can to get us.

As believers, we should not be shocked when tragedy occurs; after all, the Bible tells us these things are going to happen in the last days. Still, we seem to be shocked because we often expect Satan to repeat himself. That is, we expect Satan to utilize the same tricks he used in the past. Although Satan does not have any power, he is very clever. He realizes that believers all over the world are praying against drugs, murder, and the more obvious signs of evil. Believers have to realize that Satan has new schemes, which we have not yet prepared ourselves against. He is sneaking through the back door and hurting us in ways we do not expect. He is directly targeting and seeking to destroy our spirit. Satan is not concerned with our mortal bodies; he wants our souls.

Each time America has been attacked, the media replays video footage of 'ground zero'—the buildings damaged, the death toll, etc. The real damage, however, takes place in the heart, mind, and spirit of the people. Satan understands that terrorist attacks provoke people to walk in the lust of the flesh. He knows that when tragedy occurs, it provokes anger, rage, fear, and revenge. In these end times, the world needs to seek God and begin to walk in the Spirit.

It is true that these are the last days. The signs of the times are obvious in the news, our communities, and the dynamics of our homes. In stating that these are the last days, let us be clear. We are referencing the Bible's description of the end times, the immediate period before the second coming of Christ, and the rapture—the eventual end of life on earth. The Bible speaks of the turmoil that will occur in the end of times. *"This know also, that in the last days perilous times shall come. For men shall be lovers of their own selves, covetous, boasters, proud, blasphemers, disobedient to parents, unthankful, unholy. Without natural affection, trucebreakers, false accusers, incontinent, fierce, despisers of those that are good, traitors, heady, high-minded, lovers of pleasures more than lovers of God; Having a form of godliness, but denying the power thereof"* (2 Tim. 3:1-5).

When we consider our world today—crime, weather, politics, wars, and rumors of wars, we cannot help but to acknowledge the end is near. Like a pregnant woman in labor, the earth is actually groaning and waiting for the coming of Christ. *"For I reckon that the sufferings of this present time are not worthy to be compared with the glory which shall be revealed in us. For the earnest expectation of the creature waiteth for the manifestation of the sons of God. For the creature was made subject to vanity, not willingly, but by reason of him who hath subjected the same in hope, Because the creature itself also shall be delivered from the bondage of corruption into the glorious liberty of the children of God. For we know that the whole creation groaneth and travaileth in pain together until now"* (Romans 8:18-22).

Our world is in pain; only the Savior can heal us. The unfortunate piece of all this chaos is that most of us are not ready. That is, there are not enough lovers of

God. We have not accepted Christ into our hearts as our personal Lord and Savior; we have let the pain of this world hinder us from the hope of His glorious return. Thus, our troubled world is looking to itself for redemption. *"For the wages of sin is death; but the gift of God is eternal life through Jesus Christ our Lord"* (Rom. 6:23). Consequently, when Christ does appear, many of us will not go back with Him.

There is urgency for those of us who do know God to spread the true gospel. The gospel must be preached to those who are lost regardless if it is accepted or not. God loves us and does not want anyone to be lost. *"The Lord is not slack concerning his promise, as some men count slackness; but is longsuffering to us-ward, not willing that any should perish, but that all should come to repentance"* (2 Pet. 3:9). The love of God is so powerful that He gave His son for us. *"For God so loved the world, that he gave his only begotten Son, that whosoever believeth in him should not perish, but have everlasting life"* (John 3:16).

23

Chapter II

THE FRUIT OF THE SPIRIT AND THE LUST OF THE FLESH

"Walk in the Spirit, and you will not fulfill the lust of the flesh" (Gal. 5:16). This scripture is commonly misunderstood and taken for granted. Take the first part of this sentence—walk in the Spirit. Many of us would correctly assume this passage refers to the Holy Spirit. However, we do not understand the reason we are directed in the Word of God to walk in the Spirit. The passage discusses God's requirement that we walk in the Spirit to avoid fulfilling the lust of the flesh. Furthermore, the ways in which God has commanded believers to walk in are not humanly possible in our flesh. For example, a very basic requirement of God is that we love our neighbors as we love our self. Many of us have difficulty with this very basic requirement. Not to mention, there are countless further complex requirements of God which are difficult for us to carry out in our own strength. We are told to walk in the Spirit so we can fulfill God's commandments, and He can get the glory out of our life. Unless we walk in the Spirit and the power of the Holy Ghost, our flesh will be in control. Our flesh is naturally inclined to hatred, malice, un-forgiveness, murder, and all of the bad things that make our life miserable.

"Now the works of the flesh are manifest, which are these; Adultery, fornication, uncleanness, lasciviousness, idolatry, witchcraft, hatred, variance, emulations, wrath, strife, seditions, heresies, envyings, murders, drunkenness, revellings, and such like: of the which I tell you before, as I have also told you in time past, that they which do such things shall not inherit the kingdom of God" (Gal. 5:19-21). The human flesh naturally longs for hatred, strife, fits of wrath, drunkenness, and murders. Our bodies' natural instinct is to respond to confusion by taking on and performing the lust of the flesh. It is like an animal's instinct to the sound and smell of prey. The animal wants it, longs for it, and it will do anything to capture it—so will our human flesh do anything to fulfill its lust.

Lust creates further lust. When we begin to fulfill the lust of the flesh, our beings become comfortable, and thus, we are prone to develop further lust i.e. hatred, fear, pain, guilt, depression, etc. Our flesh longs for these things and it eventually becomes a cycle. That is why it is so hard for us to rid our self of depression and anxiety; our flesh longs for the misery produced from fulfilling the lust of the flesh. Have you ever wondered why it is so easy to forget about a happy moment, but so hard to get over a negative one? Our flesh is most comfortable in chaos. In other words, our flesh is at its most comfortable state

25

when it is fulfilling the lust of the flesh. The pain we feel, if any, comes from the longing of our bound spirit to be free. Even when we become tired of living a life of sin, we often fall right back into it as if we cannot help it. When we fulfill the lust of the flesh, we give the flesh power over our spirit; our spirit, thus, remains bound.

God created us to walk in the Spirit, but with the fall of man in the Garden of Eden, our flesh became sinful and gained power over our spirit. Because of the power of the flesh, we uncontrollably fell into sin. We were constantly offering sacrifices unto God in exchange for forgiveness of our sins—just to go back and do the same thing over again. Even God saw that we were not able to walk successfully in the Spirit; so, he sent his Son Jesus to die on the cross to pay the ultimate sacrifice for our sins. When Christ died for us, we were given back our ability to walk in the Spirit. Through Christ's sacrifice, we were given power over the flesh through salvation and the Holy Ghost. Now, just like in the Garden of Eden, we have the power to walk in the Spirit and remain connected to God. However, we have to choose to walk in the Spirit. When we walk in the Spirit, we will produce the fruit of the Spirit in our life. *"But the fruit of the Spirit is love, joy, peace, longsuffering, gentleness, goodness, faith, meekness, temperance: against such there is no law"* (Gal. 5:22-23). It is only when we walk in the Spirit that we can truly be happy and fulfilled. When we choose to walk in the Spirit, we fulfill God's original plan and become connected with our Father in Heaven.

Chapter III

SPIRITUAL WARFARE

The topic of spiritual warfare is used in various contexts within Christianity and across faiths. Although the minor details may differ, the common theme across all definitions is that spiritual warfare involves a fight. Unlike worldly warfare, spiritual warfare involves an intensity of combat that cannot be won with physical weapons.

When we are confronted with spiritual warfare, many of us lose the battle for several reasons. First, many of us are not equipped to fight because we have not yet acknowledged that we are, in fact, in a fight. Many believers go about life as if all is well. We are satisfied with our titles, fancy church suits, and going to Sunday dinner with fellow parishioners; we rarely pray or fast. Although we do a great job in following the traditions of religion, we do not have a real relationship with God. *"Wherefore the Lord said, Forasmuch as this people draw near me with their mouth, and with their lips do honour me, but have removed their heart far from me, and their fear toward me is taught by the precept of men"* (Isa. 29:13). Consequently, we are not in fellowship enough to hear from God.

Second, many of us do not know how spiritual warfare works. We are uneducated in the dynamics of spiritual warfare and ill prepared with strategy to fight Satan. Spiritual warfare is a battle between the lust of the flesh and our spirit. Therefore, when we are fighting in spiritual warfare, we must fight with spiritual weapons and not carnal ones. *"For the weapons of our warfare are not carnal, but mighty through God to the pulling down of strong holds"* (2 Cor. 10:4). In other words, guns, bombs, and spears will not prove useful in spiritual warfare. We must fight with spiritual weapons; we must fight with the Word of God. In these last and evil days, God is telling us to fight.

Third, we often look for spiritual warfare in the most obvious areas. That is, we expect Satan to use the same tactics he used against us in the past. We look for drugs, murder, war, and other popular attacks from Satan. Satan knows that every believer in the world is praying against drugs, murder, hunger, etc. He recognizes that he must come up with new tactics. Satan's desire is to kill our spirit and eventually steal our souls. He does not play fair and we have to be prepared and ready to fight.

Consider Bobby. He knows a murderer is coming for his family. After all, this same killer has hit everyone else in Bobby's neighborhood. In addition, Bobby has something the killer wants. According to evidence from the previous murders, the culprit has entered each home through the front door with a gun. Hearing this information, Bobby hides his family, stands by the front door, and waits for the killer to approach. Bobby is well prepared with guns and even has police on watch. As time passes, Bobby becomes fatigued and decides to go into the refrigerator for a glass of lemonade. After a few more hours of waiting, Bobby starts to feel a pain in his stomach and suddenly falls dead to the ground. Bobby was unaware that while he was hiding his family and taking other necessary precautions, the murderer had come in through the window of his home and poisoned the lemonade. At this point, the guns in Bobby's hand were no use against the killer who had now taken what he wanted.

We must regard spiritual warfare in this same way. We must be aware and alert—knowing that Satan is not coming in the way we expect him to. Why should he? Satan is going to attempt to seize us in ways we least expect. Actually, the ideal area for Satan to attack us in is the place we think we have it all together and know it all. He is going to attack us in the area of our life that we are less likely to trust God and more inclined to handle things on our own—based on our own strength.

In these last days, we must walk in the Spirit and be sensitive to the Father's will for our life. *"Be sober-minded; be watchful. Your adversary the devil prowls around like a roaring lion, seeking someone to devour"* (1 Pet. 5:8). Very importantly, we cannot think for one moment that our flesh is skilled enough to handle the tactics of Satan. *"For though we walk in the flesh, we do not war after the flesh: For the weapons of our warfare are not carnal, but mighty through God to the pulling down of strong holds; Casting down imaginations, and every high thing that exalteth itself against the knowledge of God, and bringing into captivity every thought to the obedience of Christ."* (2 Cor. 10:3-4).

The Bible speaks of spiritual warfare in this manner, *"For we do not wrestle against flesh and blood, but against the rulers, against the authorities, against the cosmic powers over this present darkness, and against the spiritual forces of evil in the heavenly places"* (Eph. 6:12). Spiritual warfare is a battle of the lust of our flesh against our spirit. Our spirit desires reunification with the Father as in the beginning of time. When walking in the Spirit, we will produce the fruit of the Spirit, which is love, joy, peace, longsuffering, gentleness, goodness, faith, meekness, and temperance. These are not only the fruit of the Spirit, but also the attributes of God.

Spiritual warfare occurs because our flesh has natural attributes opposite that of the fruit of the Spirit; these are the lust of the flesh. There are many situations in life, which cause a struggle to develop between our spirit and our flesh. During our most vulnerable moments and seasons of life, Satan sneaks in and attempts to destroy our spirit. *"The thief cometh not, but for to kill steal and destroy"* (John 10:10). That is, Satan strategically comes into our atmosphere when we are weak for no other reason than to kill, steal, and destroy our spirit. He wants to destroy our ability to walk in the Spirit and produce the fruit of the Spirit, which is love, joy, peace, longsuffering, gentleness, goodness, faith, meekness, and temperance. Satan is not concerned with our natural flesh, except to the extent that he wants the lust of the flesh to win over our spirit. *"For though we walk in the flesh, we are not waging war according to the flesh"* (2 Cor. 10:3). That is why in the midst of turmoil in our world, Satan is unconcerned with the loss of life or blood spill; people are killing people as if it is no big deal. Satan's sole desire is to steal the souls of the lives lost and kill the spirit of those who remain. Instead of love, joy, and peace, Satan wants us to follow the lust of the flesh. Satan knows that when tragedy strikes, we are overcome with feelings of fear, hatred, fits of wrath, strife, and other lust of the flesh. Satan is very pleased to know that people everywhere, even children, are scared to the point that they do not feel safe; their vision of living a long and full life is blemished. Still, there is hope; God says, *"I come that they might have life, and that they may have it more abundantly"* (John 10:10).

As believers, we must always keep in mind the end of the story. There is no other matter known to human-kind, besides the gospel of Jesus Christ, that we are privileged to know the future. In the end, our flesh and its lust will pass away; our spirit will remain alive and will be reunited with our Father in heaven.

Chapter IV

LOVE AND RELATIONSHIPS

S piritual warfare often comes in the form of a distraction. A distraction is an object, person, state, or idea used to divert our attention and get us off track. Let us consider two very real characteristics of distractions. First, when we consider distractions, we often imagine something obvious—something we can see, and will know exactly what it is doing to us. However, distractions are most often very subtle. That is, they present almost unnoticed. Distractions are very dangerous when it comes to the will of God. In actuality, we commonly overlook distractions because we cannot directly identify what we are being distracted away from. In spiritual warfare, the distraction is not so much physically pulling us in another direction, but it takes our attention away from God just enough so that we are unable to hear Him say to us, "Move, stop, speak, go...NOW." For many of us, our distraction comes to deter us from our purpose or some God-given assignment that will likely have a powerful impact on the kingdom of God.

Second, usually our distraction attacks us in an area where there is potential for us to become desperate for things to work out a certain way. We start to doubt God's ability to handle the situation. Said another way, in spiritual warfare, the distraction is often presented in an area of our life that we are inclined to handle on our own.

One of the primary areas that Satan targets is love and relationships. This tactic is one of Satan's preferred targets because love is a very spiritual matter, but if not handled properly can become a battle of the flesh. It is no secret we all want to be loved and in relationships. God designed us to be in love. The Bible says that we can be rich in houses and land, sing like angels and have all types of gifts, but if we do not have love, we have nothing. *"Though I speak with the tongues of men and of angels, and have not charity, I am become as sounding brass, or a tinkling cymbal. And though I have the gift of prophecy, and understand all mysteries, and all knowledge; and though I have all faith, so that I could remove mountains, and have not charity, I am nothing. And though I bestow all my goods to feed the poor, and though I give my body to be burned, and have not charity, it profiteth me nothing"* (1 Cor. 13:1-3). This specific passage references our general love for our community—brotherly love, but can also be applied to romantic love. At the creation of humankind, God himself realized that man should not be alone. Despite

33

all the animals and tasks given to Adam, he was still alone. There was something left unfulfilled in him. He needed more than animal companionship; he in fact needed sexual intimacy. He needed another human who would be like him, but also different in the way that would complement his physical structure and meet his sexual needs. God was so very careful in his creation of Adam's mate.

The creation of woman validates the fact that it is not God's desire for us to be alone. The design of woman was exclusive. Women were purposefully created to be in an intimate, sexual, and romantic relationship with a man. When we become lonely, however, we tend to blame God for our loneliness. That is, we start to suppose in our minds that it is God's desire for us to be alone. That presumption is false; it is not God's desire for us to be alone. Women were created to love and be in a sexual relationship. That is why we so strongly long for love and often feel depressed when we are not in a romantic relationship.

As well, many of us find difficulty pursuing our purpose in life because we lack a relationship to keep us grounded. There is something about being in a healthy relationship that allows for clarity in our thinking processes, creativity in our work, and ease in our spirit. This ease and contentment comes from and through having a spiritual covering. Even if our spouse is not living the spiritual life we want him to, he still provides a covering for us. The covering is especially strong when our spouse is a believer. Although pursuing our purpose does not mandate being in a relationship, the significance of being in a healthy relationship is that we have a spiritual covering while pursuing our purpose. In a healthy relationship, we are free to fulfill our calling because we are equally yoked with a believer who realizes the specific benefits of being on one accord and the impact it will have on the kingdom.

What does the Bible say about love? The Bible ascribes to the topic of romantic love numerous times. The book of the Song of Solomon, for example, describes the intimate details of King Solomon's romance and lovemaking with his mate, and her love back to him. The book consists of love letters detailing the affections of their love and descriptions of their sexual performance and intimacy within their relationship.

> *"Let him kiss me with the kisses of his mouth: for thy love is better than wine." "I am the rose of Sharon, and the lily of the valleys. As the lily among thorns, so is my love among the daughters. As the apple tree among the trees of the wood, so is my beloved among the sons. I sat down under his shadow with great delight, and his fruit was sweet to my taste. He brought me to the banqueting house, and his banner over me was love. Stay me with flagons, comfort me with apples: for I am sick of love. His left hand is under my head, and his right hand doth embrace me." "Behold, thou art*

35

fair, my love; behold, thou art fair; thou hast doves' eyes within thy locks: thy hair is as a flock of goats, that appear from mount Gilead. Thy teeth are like a flock of sheep that are even shorn, which came up from the washing; whereof every one bear twins, and none is barren among them. Thy lips are like a thread of scarlet, and thy speech is comely: thy temples are like a piece of a pomegranate within thy locks. Thy neck is like the tower of David builded for an armoury, whereon there hang a thousand bucklers, all shields of mighty men. Thy two breasts are like two young roes that are twins, which feed among the lilies. Until the day break, and the shadows flee away, I will get me to the mountain of myrrh, and to the hill of frankincense. Thou art all fair, my love; there is no spot in thee" (excerpts from the Book of Solomon, KJV)

Love is a very natural, God ordained phenomenon. *"Marriage is honorable and the bed is undefiled"* (Heb. 13:4). Our desire to be in a relationship and be in love is part of our design; there is no shame in it. No one should ever convince us, nor should we convince our self that it is not normal to want to be in love; we should deeply desire love. We should imagine our self being in a relationship. There is nothing maladaptive in fantasizing about being married and having a family.

Still, if love is so precious and right, why have so many of us been hurt by love? This dilemma arises when we become so desperate for love and mistake lust for love. We fall for something that mimics love, but in actuality is only an imitation with no longevity or commitment. *"Love suffereth long, and is kind; love envieth not; love vaunteth not itself, is not puffed up, Doth not behave itself unseemly, seeketh not her own, is not easily provoked, thinketh no evil; Rejoiceth not in iniquity, but rejoiceth in the truth; Beareth all things, believeth all things, hopeth all things, endureth all things"* (1 Cor. 13:4-7). The dilemma extends further when we become willing to compromise the well-being of our spirit for the sake of being in a relationship. Knowing what true love is and being able to wait for it, saves us from heartbreak, manipulation, and strife. If we are in a relationship and we have love, we have everything. On the other hand, if we are in a relationship and we do not have love, we have nothing.

Chapter V

UNEQUALLY YOKED

W hen we become too desperate for love and relationships, we attempt to manipulate love into our life. Instead of waiting on God, we go and try to make love happen in our own timing instead of God's timing. The importance of waiting on God is that when He finally sends love to us, we can be confident to know it is true and sincere. God's love is without chaos and we can find peace in it. When we try to force love into our life, we usually find our self in a chaotic circumstance.

Take for example, Samson in the Bible, who attempted to manipulate love with Delilah. Samson saw Delilah and fell in love with her. Samson was warned by his family not to go after someone who was an outsider. His family could not put a finger on what it was about Delilah they did not like, nor could they foresee how the relationship would play out. They knew Delilah was not equally yoked with Samson and did not know the ways of the Lord. Deep down Samson's family knew that, although Delilah was beautiful, she could not really understand Samson's anointing and God-given gifts. Samson was blinded by his lust; he could not see Delilah for who she really was. Samson's disobedience to God and his involvement in an unequally yoked relationship ended in betrayal and death.

"Be ye not unequally yoked together with unbelievers. For what fellowship hath righteousness with unrighteousness? And what communion hath light with darkness" (2 Cor. 6:14). Many of us take this scripture for granted, but disobedience to this command is the gateway for spiritual warfare into our life—through our love and relationships. We become so desperate to be in a relationship that we are willing to be unequally yoked with an unbeliever. If we can be truthful, we often know very well that the person we are pursuing is not equally yoked with us, but in the back of our minds, we naively think we can change him. When we become unequally yoked with an unbeliever, there is nothing we can do or say to change him. We begin to justify our wrongdoing and our disobedience to God. Although we may not want to admit we are getting our self into trouble, Satan knows we are being set up for a fall.

Strangely, it is very simple to get into an unequally yoked relationship, but very difficult to get out of it. When we become involved in an unequally yoked relationship, we offer the flesh power over our spirit. We begin to walk in the lust of the flesh. Even if we have not yet entered into sexual sin, we are still walking in the lust of the flesh in that relationship because of our disobedience to God. Lust of the flesh is more than sexual

39

intercourse. *"Now the works of the flesh are manifest, which are these; Adultery, fornication, uncleanness, lasciviousness, Idolatry, witchcraft, hatred, variance, emulations, wrath, strife, seditions, heresies, envyings, murders, drunkenness, revellings, and such like"* (Gal. 5:19-21). Over time, we find our self miserable in the relationship, and unable to get out of it because of the power we have given to our flesh. The relationship eventually becomes sexual and a soul tie is created. That is, because sexual intimacy is so very strong, it creates a very deep attachment that extends beyond physical attachment into the emotional and mental components of our partner's being. The soul tie creates blinders over our eyes and impairs our better judgment; we are not able to see the truth until it is too late. A soul tie is very difficult to break because of the lust of our flesh and because we were not created to be with multiple sexual partners. Even when we want to leave the relationship, we lack the spiritual strength to do so. Our mind tells us to leave, but our flesh is now too connected. We find our self embarrassed, powerless, hopeless, walking on eggshells, tense, and in emotional pain—all because we are unequally yoked. That is, we want to leave because our spirit is hurting, but because we have given our flesh power over our spirit, we do not have the wherewithal to leave. We are stuck in an unhealthy relationship.

In the story of Samson and Delilah, Delilah repeatedly deceived and manipulated Samson. She asked him on more than one occasion to disclose to her the secret of his strength, and each time she betrayed him and attempted to hurt him. Although he knew she could not be trusted and did not have his best interest at heart, Samson remained with Delilah. Eventually Samson told Delilah the true source of his strength. He thought that by telling her the intimate details of his life, she would love him more and would not betray him. In disclosing to Delilah the truth of his strength, Samson disobeyed God and eventually lost his life.

Why is it so hard to leave an unhealthy relationship? The answer is—because our flesh longs for the attributes that accompany an unhealthy relationship. Our flesh longs for hatred, discord, jealousy, fits of rage, envy, and drunkenness. In the beginning of the relationship, we thought it was so cute and innocent, but in reality, it was a trick from Satan. We are now in spiritual warfare and Satan wants to break our spirit. That is why there are so many abusive relationships and marriages, heart-breaking divorces, and people living in mental anguish; it is because we are in unequally yoked relationships. These are in fact distractions to us walking in the Spirit and producing the fruit of the Spirit. The Bible says, *"Do not be unequally yoked with unbelievers"* (2 Cor. 6:14). If we are walking in the Spirit, then we need to be in fellowship, covenant, and partnership with someone who also walks in the Spirit. *"Can two walk together, except they be agreed"* (Amos 3:3)?

Still, despite Samson's disobedience to God in marrying Delilah, it was all in God's plan.

"Then his father and his mother said unto him, Is there never a woman among the daughters of thy brethren, or among all my people, that thou goest to take a wife of the uncircumcised Philistines? And Samson said unto his father, Get her for me; for she pleaseth me well. But his father and his mother knew not that it was of the LORD, that he sought an occasion against the Philistines: for at that time the Philistines had dominion over Israel" (Judges 14:3-4).

Despite the way the situation looks, we have to trust God. Samson and his family did not know that God was using the circumstances and Samson's condition to defeat the Philistines. God is able to take a situation that was meant for our bad and turn it around for our good. Even when we are out of His will, God is able to spin things around for our good and His glory. As the story goes, after Delilah cut off Samson's hair, she took out his eyeballs so he could not see and delivered him into the hands of her people, the Philistines. Once the Philistines had Samson bound, they decided to mock him. They brought him into a party for all of the Philistine officials; they scoffed at him and everything he had been through. Delilah was very proud of her accomplishments. She had taken everything Samson had and now he was helpless. It was at Samson's most desperate point that he cried out to God.

"And Samson called unto the LORD, and said, O Lord God, remember me, I pray thee, and strengthen me, I pray thee, only this once, O God, that I may be at once avenged of the Philistines for my two eyes. And Samson took hold of the two middle pillars upon which the house stood, and on which it was borne up, of the one with his right hand, and of the other with his left. And Samson said, Let me die with the Philistines. And he bowed himself with all his might; and the house fell upon the lords, and upon all the people that were therein. So the dead which he slew at his death were more than they which he slew in his life" (Judges 16:28-30).

Despite the mistakes he made, God was able to get the glory out of Samson's life. "To trust God means to understand that He will never allow the enemy to gain total victory over our life" (Scott, 2009).

Chapter VI

CATEGORIZING ABUSE

A broad definition of abuse is 'severe misuse or mistreatment that injures or damages a person.' Abuse subjects us to treatment that is wrong and unbeneficial to our mind, body, and spirit. When we discuss abuse, we most often reference physical and/ or sexual abuse. Physical abuse refers to the malicious wounding of a person's physical body. Sexual abuse refers to unwanted sexual activity or use of someone's body—usually involving threats, force, and intimidation. All over the world, men, women, and children are tortured through physical and sexual abuse. Many victims are hospitalized, and unfortunately, some even die because of such malicious wounding.

Covert and Overt Abuse

Abuse can be separated into two distinct categories— covert and overt. Overt abuse is direct and straightforward. That is, with overt abuse, we are going to know without a doubt we are being abused. We notice feelings of depression and fear, and are able to trace our negative feelings directly back to the abuse we are experiencing. An example of overt abuse would be our abuser belittling us in public, calling us out of our name, or telling us we are worthless. Being physically beaten and raped are obvious examples of overt abuse. When we are beaten, there is no mistake or question in our mind that we are being abused; we see, feel, and know it. Furthermore, anyone looking in from the outside will realize that abuse is taking place.

Covert abuse is less direct and less obvious than overt abuse. Still, despite covert abuse being less direct, covert abuse is just as damaging as overt abuse, if not more. Covert abuse is more subtle than overt abuse. That is, covert abuse occurs in such a way that if we are not paying attention to our feelings and mood, we may not notice that abuse is taking place. Emotional abuse is considered a covert form of abuse. A good example of covert abuse is being ignored, manipulated, or lied to. These are all characteristics of emotional abuse. Being ignored, especially by someone who should be paying attention to us, overtime, will make us feel as if we do not exist. It makes us feel as if our value to our partner is little to none. Emotional abuse is often over-looked because we rarely realize it is happening.

Battle of the Sexes

Because most men are physically stronger than women, we are often at a disadvantage when physical abuse becomes a factor in a relationship. Most men, no matter how short or tall they stand in stature are naturally stronger than women. Even little boys, although they are not fully grown, can already begin to feel their strength by the time they are 10 or 11. The strength of a man grows at an incredible rate. They can become strong so fast that they may feel a sense of power and even invincibility—as if nothing can hurt them. This sense of power can cause men to handle their emotions in a physically harmful way.

Take for example; Terrance knows he is very strong physically. He used his physical strength to intimidate everyone in his life. If someone hurt his feelings, he handled the situation with his muscles instead of working it out sensibly, through proper communication and problem solving. Terrance is currently serving time for issues with domestic violence. He never learned how to control his anger; he became used to intimidating everyone with his muscles. When he married his high school sweet heart, he tried to handle his marital problems with intimidation. Each time his wife attempted to talk to him about her feelings, he would become frustrated, tell her she was too emotional, and would eventually hit her. Terrance loved his wife very much, but was unable to handle neither her emotions nor his own. Sometimes, abuse starts with a person being unable to handle his emotions.

There is great controversy over the idea that women are the weaker vessel. According to the Bible, women are the weaker vessel and the man is the head of the household. This is a tough pill for many women to swallow—especially in lieu of the dynamics of family structure in our modern day society. There is an increasing amount of single parent households where women have to fulfill the role of the man and still be the woman. However, this dynamic of family structure was never how God designed the family to be. Just because we believe we are doing everything a man is supposed to be doing does not mean we are just as strong as a man is. We are still the weaker vessel. The phenomenon of women being the 'weaker vessel' refers not only to the physical ratios between male and female strength, but extends to emotional and spiritual aspects, also. God gave us women wisdom and virtue to be strong and take care of our business, but He never meant for us to be ahead of or replace the man. When we are in a healthy relationship, we naturally succumb to the physical, emotional, and spiritual strength of the man. We are naturally inclined to let him take the lead because that is how God designed us. This does not mean that we are to be a footstool. In the beginning, God created women to complement the strength and needs of the man through our love and affection. God designed men to be the covering for women—physically, emotionally, and spiritually.

Chapter VII

EMOTIONAL ABUSE

When we admit we have been abused in a romantic relationship, the first thing people assume is that we were physically abused. We have to remember that abuse comes in many forms i.e. mental, verbal, emotional, physical, sexual, etc. Abuse can even be spiritual. One common long-term effect of the above-mentioned forms of abuse is emotional damage. That is, although emotional abuse comes as a category of abuse by itself, the other forms of abuse all involve a component of emotional abuse.

**Let us be clear and say, there is no worse form of abuse or torment than that of sexual abuse. As we discuss abuse, we do not want to undermine the devastation of rape, or the experiences of anyone who has had such a travesty occur. The impact of sexual abuse is apparent on all levels—physical, spiritual, mental, and emotional. Unlike a romantic relationship, in which we invite a person into our heart and spirit, rape involves a direct, unwelcomed invasion of our body, mind, and spirit. Unfortunately, for many victims, their sexual abuse goes unreported or authorities do not believe them. Regardless, the effects are devastating and long lasting. To make certain that justice is served, police, court officials, doctors, social workers, teachers, and any other parties involved in investigating and helping victims should consider delving into the deeper evidences of sexual abuse. That is, no matter how many rape kits and interviews are performed, the real evidence of sexual abuse is the damage to the spirit.

Emotional abuse, also referred to as psychological abuse is described as,

> *"Mistreatment which subjects the victim to one or more of the following with malicious intent: humiliation and degrading, discounting, distorting and negating, accusing and blaming, isolating, withholding affection and emotional support, withholding financial resources, dismissive, disapproving and contemptuous looks, comments and behaviors, threatening harm to an individual's pets, possessions and persons, and silence" (Yerkes, 2007).*

Although characteristics of emotional abuse may seem insignificant to some, when we suffer these things over long periods of time, our mind, body and spirit are negatively impacted. The impact of emotional abuse is long lasting and devastating.

Humiliation and Degrading

Humiliation and degrading in an emotionally abusive relationship involve embarrassing, putting down and demeaning us through acts such as arguing in public, persistent flirting with other women, cheating, etc. Humiliation and degrading make us feel worthless. This is because we are not the only ones who know about it. That is, our family, friends, co-workers, and even random strangers can see what is wrong in the relationship. The abuser has no shame in his actions towards us. If we are educated, the abuser may try to make us feel we are ignorant by mocking us in front of his friends. The abuser may tell our very private information, or may point out our faults and mistakes to others. Ironically, the source of the humiliation and degradation is the abuser's fear of us. That is, the abuser is intimidated by our success and character. Nevertheless, humiliation and degrading have devastating effects on our peace of mind.

Discounting, Distorting, and Negating

An abuser is much like a good liar. A good liar will try to make us feel as if we are the one lying—that is how strong and potent the spirit of lying is. Abusers are usually very good liars and strong manipulators. Take for example, most of us can look into the sky and agree the sky is blue. However, for no apparent reason, an abuser will discount, distort, and negate everything we are saying; he will question and attack our words and thoughts so well that we may actually question if the sky is blue. This is the ongoing effect of abuse; it makes us question not only our self-worth, but also our intelligence, beauty, knowledge, etc. Emotional abuse causes us to question every quality we have.

Accusing and Blaming

In an abusive relationship, there is no attempt at reconciliation. The abuser accuses and blames us for everything. That is, the abuser has so much pride that he will never apologize for his wrongdoings. He will allow an issue to linger knowing very well he is wrong. In order to move forward, we often have to decide to let the issue go and act as if nothing happened—because we know the abuser is never going to apologize. We may even find our self apologizing just to regain peace in the home.

Conversely, in a healthy relationship, our partner will attempt to settle the argument. The Holy Spirit will convict him and he will apologize. He will not only apologize, but will validate our feelings, will seek out ways to regain our trust, and will do his very best not to make the same mistake again. On the other hand, an abuser will allow us to sulk in our negative feelings. An abuser will try to convince us that we are crazy and should not be having such feelings. This is emotional abuse.

Take for example, Elizabeth and her husband, Tim. At the company picnic, Tim spent several hours walking, talking, and laughing with a strange woman while Elizabeth watched their three children play. Tim never introduced Elizabeth to the woman and never came to check on Elizabeth and the children. As a result, Elizabeth felt ignored and disrespected. She knew deep down that Tim's actions were wrong. When Elizabeth told Tim how she felt about his behavior, he acted as if he did nothing wrong. During the argument, Tim turned the situation around and blamed Elizabeth. He became rude and disrespectful; he tried to convince her that she was crazy. Tim told Elizabeth that she should not have been so self-conscious and should have come over and introduced herself to his friend—whom he said was just a coworker. Tim allowed the issue to linger. He tried to convince Elizabeth that the argument was her fault—she should not have been so insecure and had no reason to feel the way she did. Although Tim knew he was wrong, he never went back to his wife to apologize; he never took the time to validate her feelings. That is, if Tim had been truthful and admitted fault, Elizabeth would have felt better and would have known her feelings were valid. After days of Tim accusing and blaming Elizabeth, she eventually apologized to him for being so insecure. Months later, Elizabeth found out that her husband and the strange woman had been having an affair. She became angry with herself for letting him convince her that she was wrong. Let us be clear, in an emotionally abusive relationship, the abuser will never validate our feelings; he will accuse and blame us for everything although he knows he is wrong.

Isolating

In an emotionally abusive relationship, isolation involves taking us away from the people who love us, can protect us, and very importantly, can look into our spirit and discern that something is wrong. Isolation does not occur immediately. Instead, it is a gradual process and can begin in various ways. The abuser makes excuses not to accompany us to family functions, work events, and even church; he may pretend to be sick or too tired. Overtime, we begin to feel guilty for leaving him home alone, so we stay home with him.

Another means to isolation is when the abuser points out things he does not like about our family, friends and coworkers. He may try to convince us that our loved ones are bad influences on our marriage and us. The abuser also may accuse us of putting other people in front of him. The abuser may even misuse Biblical scriptures to back his reasoning to keep us from our loved ones. The truth of the matter is, the abuser does not want us to be around the people we love, the people that will speak up for us, and the people that will protect us—from him.

Withholding Affection and Emotional Support

Emotional abuse can cause us to question our sexuality. In this discussion, we are not referring to sexual preference—although, many members of the LGBT (lesbian, gay, bisexual, and transgender) population will admit they were victims of abuse. Instead, sexuality in this context refers to the sense of being sexual or feeling sexy. In an emotionally abusive relationship, the abuser will withhold love and affection from us. That is, the abuser will intentionally withhold intimacy as a means and attempt to hurt and control us. He knows very well that, at the end of the day, all we really want is to be held. The abuser knows that above all else, we value his affection. He does not have to give us lots of money or extravagant gifts to gain our loyalty. We do not require a luxurious house or fancy car, but we do crave his love and affection. The abuser knows affection is central to our wellbeing and will withhold it maliciously. Affection costs nothing, and comes naturally to those who are truly in love. The abuser knows that withholding affection is the only way to really hurt us.

When affection is withheld for lengthy periods, we begin to question our sexuality. We ask questions such as, "Am I beautiful? Am I satisfying him? Am I what he really needs?" Emotional abuse de-feminizes a woman, and likewise, emotional abuse attacks at a man's masculinity. Specifically, when we are withheld affection and sexual intimacy, overtime, we do not feel so much like a woman anymore. Yes, we still are a woman, but in terms of our physical beauty and sexuality, we feel as if we are lacking. In the book of the Song of Solomon, King Solomon writes love songs about the beauty of a woman. Several other passages throughout the Bible reference the physical, sexual, and spiritual beauty of a woman. Emotional abuse takes from us the spirit, femininity, and God-given emotional gifts that we bring to the table. God designed us and deposited into us an energy and indescribable freshness that is distinct from that of a man; he made us special. Emotional abuse punctures our inner spirit so that we no longer feel as special as we should. We are a good thing; God made us that way. *"He that finds a wife finds a good thing"* (Prov. 18:22). Emotional abuse pries at that 'good thing.'

Withholding Financial Resources

In a healthy marriage, the finances are most often shared. That is, it does not matter how much is earned by either spouse, the sum of it belongs to the family as a whole. Each couple may have their own way of sharing the funds, but if a need or desire arises, the couple works together. This is true even if one spouse is the home-maker, breadwinner, or if one is unemployed for a period; any money earned is freely shared with the family.

In an emotionally abusive relationship, the abuser has difficulty sharing his earnings. He tends to think his money should remain in his control. This becomes especially frustrating when the abuser makes the majority of the money. He will withhold money and question every expense and purchase that we make. If we need or desire any money outside of the bills due, the abuser will deny us, but will not hesitate to buy anything he desires. This puts us in a position to beg for money and possibly compromise our self-worth.

Ironically, this form of emotional abuse occurs even if the abuser is not the primary breadwinner. Even if he makes a significantly lesser amount of money than we do, he will still try to control us by not contributing his earnings to the household. This creates unnecessary pressure since the money earned could significantly help.

Once again, we find our self begging him to help with the household expenses. Nevertheless, the abuser insists on spending his earnings on his wants instead of the needs of the family. The abuser uses guilt and manipulation as a tactic to continue this selfish and unhealthy control.

Dismissive, Disapproving, and Contemptuous Looks, Comments, and Behaviors

Similar to other characteristics of emotional abuse, dismissive, disapproving, and contemptuous looks, comments and behaviors cause us to question our self. Such vices are considered indirect forms of negative communication. That is, they portray negativity, but not in a direct way so that we can be sure of our abuser's thoughts and opinions. When confronted, the abuser can easily deny he was making a nasty face or looking a certain way at us. He can deny that his comment was meant in a negative way. Because of our uncertainty of the abuser's feelings towards us, we question and ultimately blame our self.

Threatening Harm to an Individual's Pets, Possessions and Persons

The overall purpose of threatening is to create fear and control. Threatening causes us to question our wellbeing and safety. In an emotionally abusive relationship, threatening in any manner causes us to walk on eggshells. The abuser wants us to see him as powerful, mighty, and unpredictable. Although the abuser may never do us physical harm, he alludes to the idea through his comments and gestures. An abuser will talk about violent acts in his past or refer to people in his life who may actually carry out such threats—just to intimidate us. The abuser will perform seemingly harmless acts to create fear in us such as throwing a glass of water on us, breaking or destroying our personal items, throwing our food out the window, or driving dangerously while we and/or our children are in the car. When children are involved, the abuser will try to use them against us. He may threaten to take them away to create fear in us or may even take them for long periods without letting us know where they are—just so we can worry. The abuser is desperate to control us through fear.

Silence

Silence is a subtle sign of emotional abuse. That is, if we are not paying attention to our feelings, our thinking patterns, or our emotions, we may not consider it abuse. Silence can be good for us; we all need time to think and relax. Nothing is wrong with coming home from work or school, and taking a few minutes in our room or quiet place, to lie down and meditate. In a healthy relationship, our partner understands our need for space. However, when silence is used as a means of abuse by a partner, it creates questions. We naturally wonder if something is wrong with him. We immediately want to fix whatever is wrong so that he is not suffering in any way. When the silence continues, we start to question if we did something wrong; we become nervous and edgy because we do not understand why he is being silent. Eventually, we start to blame our self.

The difference between silence in a healthy relationship and an emotionally abusive relationship is that our loving partner will not allow silence to last too long. In a healthy relationship, our partner is going to let us know exactly why he is choosing to be quiet. That is, he is going to give us details of what is wrong or not wrong with him. Furthermore, when our partner responds to our questions, his answers are going to make sense. He is going to explain his silence in ways we understand, using timelines and examples, if necessary. He will make sure we know exactly what is going on with him—and he will do it in love.

In an abusive relationship, the abuser does not readily answer our questions about what is bothering him; he leaves us to sulk in our feelings of uncertainty. Because the abuser does not make efforts to put our minds at ease, our questions and feelings of uncertainty quickly develop into anxiety, decreased self-worth, low self-esteem, and powerlessness.

Chapter VIII

WOUNDED SELF-WORTH AND POWERLESSNESS

Wounded Self Worth

E motional abuse creates a wounded sense of self-worth. We have difficulty believing in our self; we do not believe we deserve anything good. We exaggerate our abuser's power and our own helplessness. Our victim mentality makes the abuser seem very powerful, great, talented, and skilled. In our mind, the abuser is in control; he has everything and we should feel lucky to have him in our life. The mildew from emotional abuse renders us helpless. Take a moment to compare the giant from "Jack and the Beanstalk" to a small helpless child; this is the distorted image we create within our self as a result of emotional abuse.

Unfortunately, our shattered self worth extends beyond our relationship with the abuser; it extends into our perceptions and relationships with others i.e., how we see our loved ones, teachers, peers, employers, and even complete strangers. Emotional abuse affects our social skills and our desire to go out and be around people; we constantly feel as if we are less worthy than everyone else around us is. Because we are so used to being hurt and criticized by our abuser, we tend to think everyone else in our world is also trying to hurt us. This is also a reason why it is so difficult for us to get into relationships after the emotional abuse. It is not that we are not beautiful or attractive, but we do not consider our self good enough.

Powerlessness

One of the most devastating effects of emotional abuse is that it causes us to feel powerless. When considering abuse, children are unable to defend themselves and put an end to their abuse. Unlike children, adults suffering from emotional abuse do have the power to put an end to it. We actually have the power to say, "No." The difficulty is that, very often, once we are abused, we assume a state of powerlessness. That is, we take on a childlike mentality in which we do not feel we have the power to end the abuse; we feel helpless. We feel as if we need someone else to come in and save us from the hands of our abuser. However, we are adults and we have the God-given power to end our abuse.

Emotional abuse causes us to feel as if we lack the power to control our situation, circumstances, and future. Emotional abuse makes us feel inadequate—as if we do not have the skills or ability to make good things happen. We lack the confidence of knowing we are a good person or that we deserve anything good. The powerlessness yielded from emotional abuse extends into various areas of our life. It makes us feel afraid— thinking it will happen again, unable to live life, or go about a normal routine. It extends into our personal thoughts, relationships with others, productivity as students and employees, parenting skills, ability to believe positively, and much more. Unfortunately, this state of powerlessness does not stop when the emotional abuse stops. The powerlessness eventually becomes our norm; it becomes a way of living for us. Despite the longevity of emotional abuse, there is hope. If we can regain our sense of power, then we can muster up the ability and confidence to put an end to the emotional abuse in our life, and move forward.

Deciphering an Abusive Relationship

How do we distinguish emotional abuse? How do we determine if the problems in our relationship are normal or if we are being emotionally abused? Every argument or disagreement is not emotional abuse. We all have disagreements with our partners. Disagreements are part of the normal growing process for any relationship. As well, we are human and we have moments in which we say things that may hurt our partner. However, there are very distinct characteristics of abuse. Knowing them can help us discern if we are in a relationship with an abuser.

61

First, we must know and remember that emotional abuse is INTENTIONAL. That is, the abuser deliberately seeks out to hurt and tear us down. He wants to gain power and control over us. He will do anything in his power to bruise our self-worth and self-esteem. An abuser wants us to feel as if we are less worthy, less beautiful, and less deserving than he is.

Secondly, if given the opportunity, the abuser will make certain that the abuse continues. He cannot get enough of the control he has over us; he thrives on it. Take for example, silence. At first, we may just consider silence to be one of the growing pains of our relationship, but when it continues and gets worse over time, we have to realize we are involved in an emotionally abusive relationship. In a healthy relationship, over time, we begin to know our partner and recognize the dynamics of his personality. We begin to know where he is at both mentally and emotionally. We can watch him get out of the car and almost predict how his day went and his mood at the time. In an abusive relationship, even after many years, we never arrive to that level of comfort, familiarity, and friendship. We continue to walk on eggshells; the abuser may be calm and sensible in one moment and in the next instant, completely irrational. His mood, temperance, and way of doing things remain unstable and unpredictable—thus leaving us tense and anxious.

Chapter IX

A Broken Spirit, Who Can Bear?

" T he spirit of a man will sustain his infirmity, but a broken spirit who can bear" (Prov. 18:14). The worst possible danger of emotional abuse is its affect on our spirit. Emotional abuse wounds more than just the physical body; it severely wounds the spirit. Doctors may be able to mend our broken bones and bruises, but who can mend the broken spirit? We can take pain medications to alleviate the pain of physical abuse, but medications are no use for a broken spirit. Emotional abuse directly hinders and impedes our ability to walk in the Spirit and produce the fruit of the Spirit. Because of emotional abuse, we produce the lust of the flesh.

Lust Begets Lust

We hear all the time that, "hurting people hurt people." Hurting people hurt people because of emotional abuse and the lust of the flesh. *"Now the works of the flesh are manifest, which are these; adultery, fornication, uncleanness, lasciviousness, idolatry, witchcraft, hatred, variance, emulations, wrath, strife, seditions, heresies, envyings, murders, drunkenness, revellings, and such like: of the which I tell you before, as I have also told you in time past, that they which do such things shall not inherit the kingdom of God"* (Gal. 5:19-21). Take for example; wrath refers to the intentional fury and desire for revenge produced when a person becomes angry. Overtime, wrath is re-created in us in an emotional abuse. We start to seek out revenge on our abuser for the hurt we are suffering. Likewise, emulation is re-created when we start to do things to try to prove that we are better than our abuser. If we are not careful, envy, hatred, adultery, strife, and all of the above can be re-created in us as a result of suffering from emotional abuse. Ironically, unless deliverance takes place, abuse will yield the same lust in us as it does in the abuser. That is, we are at risk of becoming an abuser.

Emotional abuse wounds our ability to walk in love, joy, and peace. That is why Satan uses emotional abuse against us so often; he purposely wants us to reproduce the lust of the flesh. He wants it to become a vicious cycle. Satan wants us to be hurt and abused so that, eventually, we become the ones full of hatred. He wants us to hate our abuser and envy the life we could have had. Emotional abuse is a product of the lust of the flesh. Unfortunately, there is no good thing in our flesh and the end will be a disaster.

"For this cause shall a man leave his father and mother, and cleave to his wife; And they twain shall be one flesh: so then they are no more twain, but one flesh" (Mat. 19:5-6). When we marry, we become one with our spouse. It is important to become one with someone who is walking in the Spirit and not the lust of the flesh. *"Be ye not unequally yoked with unbelievers"* (2 Cor. 6:14). Unbelievers have not yet yielded to the Spirit, and therefore, are still subject to the lust of the flesh. Being that we are now one with them puts us at risk of also walking in the lust of the flesh.

Comparing Our Relationship to the Word of God

When things are just not right in our relationship, we have to ask our self, "In this relationship, am I able to walk in the Spirit and produce the fruit of the Spirit?" When we think we could possibly be involved in an abusive relationship, it is very important we compare our partner and our self to the Word of God.

"If we live in the Spirit, let us also walk in the Spirit. Let us not be desirous of vain glory, provoking one another, envying one another" (Gal. 5:25-26). If our partner is obeying the Word of God and the Holy Spirit, there will be peace in our relationship. If our partner is walking in the Spirit, they will produce the fruit of the Spirit. *"But the fruit of the Spirit is love, joy, peace, longsuffering, gentleness, goodness, faith, Meekness, temperance: against such there is no law. And they that are Christ's have crucified the flesh with the affections and lust"* (Gal.

5:22-24). The Word of God tells us we are *"fearfully and wonderfully made"* (Ps 139:14). *"For I know the thoughts that I think toward you, says the Lord, thoughts of peace, and not of evil, to give you an expected end"* (Jer. 29:11).

If the dynamics of our relationship resemble the lust of the flesh more than the fruit of the Spirit, it is quite possible we have an abuser on our hands. We can identify an abuser because the things he is sowing and speaking into our life on a daily basis are not in line with the Word of God. In fact, his actions directly contradict the Word of God. Instead of building us up, abusers desire to damage our sense of dignity and God-given self worth. If our partner is walking in the flesh, he is going to produce the lust of the flesh. He is going to produce *"adultery, fornication, uncleanness, lasciviousness, idolatry, witchcraft, hatred, variance, emulations, wrath, strife, seditions, heresies, envyings, murders, drunkenness, revellings, and such like"* (Gal. 5:19-21).

Principalities and Powers

"For we wrestle not against flesh and blood, but against principalities, against powers, against the rulers of the darkness of this world, against spiritual wickedness in high places" Eph. 6:12). The true enemy we are fighting is not our spouse, but it is Satan. At some point, our abuser opened up the door for Satan to use him. Satan will use anyone and anything he can. He longs to destroy our spirit and eventually steal our soul. The real

battle we are fighting is not against flesh and blood, but against principalities and powers.

Take for example, Job. Job's test was not with any particular person, nor was it because of any wrongdoing he had done. Satan himself went to God and asked for permission to test Job. Job lost his children and all of his possessions. His own wife, who knew his love for God, told him to curse God and die. Job understood that his possessions were merely things. He understood that his children did not belong to him, but were gifts from God. Job lost everything he had. Through everything he suffered, Job responded with faith and humility; he fell down and worshipped. *"Then Job arose, and rent his mantle, and shaved his head, and fell down upon the ground, and worshipped, And said, Naked came I out of my mother's womb, and naked shall I return thither: the Lord gave, and the Lord hath taken away; blessed be the name of the Lord. In all this Job sinned not, nor charged God foolishly"* (Job 1:20-22).

However, when we continue reading the book of Job, we see that Satan did not stop there. From the beginning, Satan knew the battleground would be in Job's mind. He quickly sought to attack Job's mind and damage his spirit. After Job lost his children, his possessions, and the loyalty of his wife, he was stricken with boils all over his body and was homeless. The very people he used to help, laughed, mocked, and taunted him. Through all of this, Job still did not sin. One day, Job's friends came to visit him, and although they meant well, they started speaking negativity into his mind. They questioned Job and seemingly distorted his faith in God. It was after Satan, through Job's friends, began to attack his mind that Job began to question God. He became angry and even cursed the day he was born.

Let us be very clear. It was not the loss of his children and possessions, or the boils on his own body that caused Job to become weak; it was when Satan began to attack his mind with negative thoughts that Job fell weak in his spirit. The battle is in the mind. Satan understands this principle of the mind much more than we do. Satan understands that if he can penetrate our mind, he can potentially get us. The way Satan works is, he attacks our mind with negative thoughts about our self and God's plan for our life. As we give into demonic driven thoughts, our spirit becomes weak and fails to adhere to the Word of God. This gives Satan an open door to come in and try to win the battle. However, we have to remember, *"the battle is not yours, but God's"* (2 Chron. 20:15).

That is why the Bible says, *"Let this mind be in you which is also in Christ Jesus"* (Phil. 2:5). In the midst of Job's complaining, God spoke to him out of the whirlwind. God said to Job, *"Where were you when I laid foundations of the earth? Declare, if thou hast understanding"* (Job 38:4). God essentially reminded Job that He has a right to do whatever He wants to do in our life, for his own glory. Job eventually humbled himself before God. In all he went through, Job did not sin. Because of Job's faithfulness to God, he was blessed with more than he had before. *"So the LORD blessed the latter end of Job more than his beginning"* (Job 42:12).

Much like Job, we can lose everything we own and have to live on the streets, but if we can maintain hope and faith, then we can still succeed. That is, if we can remain positive about our place in God, we can find strength to persevere. *"For I know the thoughts I have toward you, says the Lord, thoughts of peace, and not of evil, to give you an expected end"* (Job 29:11)

Darlene's Story

To anyone in an emotionally abusive relationship, you can break free. Take for example, Darlene. Darlene was in an abusive relationship, but because of her love for her husband and dedication to her vows, she would not leave the marriage. She married her husband as a virgin and they had two beautiful children together. If it had been up to Darlene, she would have stayed with her husband until death. Darlene's husband constantly put her down, isolated her from her family and friends, belittled her in public, and withheld sexual intimacy from her. Despite her beautiful figure and pleasant personality, he refused to hold her hand or acknowledge her in public. He even refused to kiss or have sex with her in the privacy of their home. Although he denied cheating, all the signs were there; he would even call and text other women while in the bed with Darlene. There was no doubt Darlene's spirit was broken and she began to question her self-worth. Despite all of this, Darlene was committed to her relationship; she was in love. Besides that, Darlene simply did not have the physical, mental, or spiritual strength to get out of such a bad relationship.

Darlene would have never left her husband; however, her father was a mighty man of God. Although he lived across the country, Darlene's father was praying and had already discerned that something was wrong. One October, while visiting Darlene, he was able to observe, first-hand, that his daughter was being treated badly. Not only that, but Darlene made excuses for her husband and blamed herself. Darlene's father was able to observe the turmoil in her marriage and the emotional abuse she had been suffering. He became fearful for his daughter's well-being and for his grandchildren. On the day he was to fly back home, Darlene's father began to pray right in front of his daughter, "Lord, my daughter is not going to leave this man. So, if he is not going to change and treat her right, I am asking you to make him leave." After the prayer, Darlene became upset with her father. With tears rolling down her face, she asked her father, "Why are you praying against my marriage?" Her father responded, "This marriage is not of God." With sincerity in his eyes, he continued, "And since you do not have the strength to leave him, I pray that he leaves you." Darlene knew that her father was a man of God and that God honored his prayers.

The trip ended, her father flew back home, and the abuse continued in Darlene's marriage. At this point in her life, Darlene feared that if the marriage ended, no one else would want her and her two small children; so she continued to put up with the abuse in her life. About a month after her father left, without warning, Darlene's husband told her that he was leaving her. Fifteen days later, Darlene took her children to a birthday party. When she came home, she saw that her husband had packed his belongings and left. Months passed and Darlene begged her husband to come back. Eventually Darlene and her husband divorced. A few weeks after the divorce, Darlene's husband called her on the phone and asked, "Why did you make me leave?"

Healing and Reconciliation

For many of us, it is very difficult to leave an abusive relationship. Our reluctance to leave is not because we are not hurting, but because we do not want people to find out what is really going on in our world, especially in the privacy of our homes. No one can judge us for that. Still, we all have to answer to God for our self; we are accountable for making the most of the time we live here on earth. If we find our self unable to worship and serve God because of the turmoil in our emotionally abusive relationship, then we are obligated, at least, to ask God for help. If we look in the mirror and cannot recognize who we are, then it is time for a change.

Darlene's story proves that prayer changes things; God is faithful and He is able to deliver us. Darlene is now a healthy, happy, and still single mother. She does not regret her experiences because they made her stronger. Darlene's worse fear had been that she would be a single parent and alone. She realizes now that leaving the marriage was the best thing she could have done for herself and her children. She is much happier now than she ever was in her marriage. Eventually, Darlene will remarry and will truly appreciate a real man and a healthy relationship. At first, Darlene did not understand God's plan. She spent a long time wondering why God did not allow her marriage to work, but ultimately, her prayer was that the will of the Lord be done in her life.

There are many testimonies from people who separated from a spouse because of abuse. During the separation period, their spouse surrendered to God and was transformed into the person God called him to be. The couples reconciled and are now living life more abundantly. This is not impossible. Pray to the Father; it is guaranteed that He hears us. We must let Him know the desires of our heart, but also be willing to accept His will for our life. God's plan may be to stay in the relationship. *"For the unbelieving husband is sanctified by the wife and the unbelieving wife is sanctified by the husband"* (1 Cor. 7:14).

Nevertheless, it is highly unlikely that the will of God is for us to stay in a physically abusive relationship in which our life is put at risk. *"What? Know ye not that your body is the temple of the Holy Ghost which is in you, which ye have of God, and ye are not your own"* (1 Cor. 6:19). God would never want us to be beaten. **If you are in a physically abusive relationship, leave now. The person you are with does not honor you nor does he honor God.**

The Progression of Sin

God never intended for us to be emotionally abused. However, for many of us to leave the relationship would mean divorce. Divorce is against many church doctrines and family standards. Besides that, the Bible does say, God hates divorce. However, there is no place in the Bible where God says He hates us because we are divorced. Divorce is never what God wants, but He allows it to happen at times because of the hardness of the heart of man. In fact, in the same passage in which He expresses his displeasure for divorce, He also expresses his scorn for those who cover up the hatred in their heart with marriage. *"For the LORD, the God of Israel, saith that he hateth putting away: for one covereth violence with his garment, saith the Lord of hosts: therefore take heed to your spirit, that ye deal not treacherously"* (Mal 2:16).

Divorce does not always have to be an option. God is very powerful. Without a doubt, He is able to come in and change the heart of the abuser towards salvation and redemption. Even so, sometimes the Holy Spirit will convict the abuser, but he will not humble his heart enough to change. *"And even as they did not like to retain God in their knowledge, God gave them over to a reprobate mind, to do those things which are not convenient"* (Rom. 1:28). This passage in Romans speaks to the reality that there is a progression of sin and those who continually disobey God can get to a point of no return, and are unable to change. When dealing with someone who has been turned over to a reprobate mind, there is nothing we can do to make him change. We have to be very careful that we do not, because of an emotionally abusive relationship, fall so deeply into sin that God turns us over to a reprobate mind also. We do not want to stay so long in an abusive relationship that we fall into disobedience. We must be sensitive to the Holy Spirit for direction. When we pray that God's will be done, we are essentially saying that we are okay with whatever He decides to do with the situation. We are giving Him full control.

Tamar's story in II Samuel is a prime example of the progression of sin and the process of emotional abuse. Her story illustrates the dynamics and effects of abuse from start to finish. Abuse always starts and ends with sin and the lust of the flesh. God does not desire for us to be abused. He wants us to live. *"I am come that they might have life, and that they might have it more abundantly"* (John 10:10).

II Samuel 13

"And it came to pass after this, that Absalom the son of David had a fair sister, whose name was Tamar; and Amnon the son of David loved her. And Amnon was so vexed, that he fell sick for his sister Tamar; for she was a virgin; and Amnon thought it hard for him to do anything to her. But Amnon had a friend, whose name was Jonadab, the son of Shimeah David's brother: and Jonadab was a very subtil man. And he said unto him, Why art thou, being the king's son, lean from day to day? wilt thou not tell me? And Amnon said unto him, I love Tamar, my brother Absalom's sister. And Jonadab said unto him, Lay thee down on thy bed, and make thyself sick: and when thy father cometh to see thee, say unto him, I pray thee, let my sister Tamar come, and give me meat, and dress the meat in my sight, that I may see it, and eat it at her hand. So Amnon lay down, and made himself sick: and when the king was come to see him, Amnon said unto the king, I pray thee, let Tamar my sister come, and make me a couple of cakes in my sight, that I may eat at her hand. Then David sent home to Tamar, saying, Go now to thy brother Amnon's house, and dress him meat. So Tamar went to her

brother Amnon's house; and he was laid down. And she took flour, and kneaded it, and made cakes in his sight, and did bake the cakes. And she took a pan, and poured them out before him; but he refused to eat. And Amnon said, Have out all men from me. And they went out every man from him. And Amnon said unto Tamar, Bring the meat into the chamber, that I may eat of thine hand. And Tamar took the cakes which she had made, and brought them into the chamber to Amnon her brother. And when she had brought them unto him to eat, he took hold of her, and said unto her, Come lie with me, my sister. And she answered him, Nay, my brother, do not force me; for no such thing ought to be done in Israel: do not thou this folly. And I, whither shall I cause my shame to go? and as for thee, thou shalt be as one of the fools in Israel. Now therefore, I pray thee, speak unto the king; for he will not withhold me from thee. Howbeit he would not hearken unto her voice: but, being stronger than she, forced her, and lay with her. Then Amnon hated her exceedingly; so that the hatred wherewith he hated her was greater than the love wherewith he had loved her. And Amnon said unto her, Arise, be gone. And she said unto him, There is no cause: this evil in sending me away is greater than the other that thou didst unto me. But he would not hearken unto her. Then he called his servant that ministered unto him, and said, Put now this woman out from me, and bolt the door after her. And she had a garment of divers colours upon her: for with such robes were the king's daughters that were virgins apparelled. Then his servant brought her out, and bolted the door after her. And Tamar put ashes on her head, and rent her garment of divers colours that was on her, and laid her hand on her head, and went on crying. And Absalom her brother said unto her, Hath Amnon thy brother been with thee? but hold now thy peace, my sister: he is thy brother; regard not this thing. So Tamar remained desolate in her brother Absalom's house."

Chapter X

TAMAR'S STORY

K ing David had a large number of sons by his wives and concubines. Amnon was the eldest son; his mother was Ahinoam. The third eldest was Absalom. Tamar was Absalom's sister; they shared the same mother—Maacah. Tamar, in addition to being beautiful, was also a virgin. Ultimately, the eldest brother, Amnon, raped his half-sister, Tamar. Although it was indeed a tragedy, the abuse Tamar suffered neither began nor ended with the rape. Similar to many of our personal stories, Tamar's suffering was not restricted to the sexual abuse that characterized her rape. As the story goes, Tamar suffered abuse on multiple levels including emotional, physical, sexual, verbal, and spiritual. More lethal than the physical and sexual turmoil she suffered, was the lasting emotional havoc of it all. The emotional abuse left her spirit shattered and in despair. A path that started out so innocently for Tamar ended in tragedy. In analyzing the story of Tamar, it is important to understand the dynamics of abuse, the mentality of the abuser, and the affects of abuse on the spirit.

The story begins with a description of the mentality of Amnon. The Bible describes Amnon as vexed. Not specifically stated in the scriptures, Amnon possibly had a mental illness; he was disturbed in his mind. Although Amnon was the eldest son of the king, by this time in the scriptures, King David had already informally decided his younger son Solomon would be succeeding him as King of Israel. This perhaps stirred up hatred and animosity in Amnon's heart towards his family and the kingdom. It is easy to fathom Amnon's sense of not being good enough to be king and even a longing for revenge. He partnered his yearning to be king with an 'I don't care' attitude about his future and about the opinions of those around him. At this point in his life, he had been disappointed and decided to do whatever he wanted without consideration for others. His hatred for himself and those around him, as well as his ability to get away with mischief (because he was the son of the king) gave him a sense of entitlement, grandiosity, and invincibility. That is, provoked by his own hurt, he began to entertain an alter personality which allowed him to feel more worthy than everyone else and entitled to anything and anyone he wanted. Amnon was beginning to lose his grip on reality; after all, his reality was very painful.

Amnon fell in love with and became obsessed with his sister, Tamar. His delusions of grandeur had impeded upon his good conscious, common sense, and ability to distinguish between right and wrong. The idea that Amnon fell in love with his sister indicated he had officially stepped outside of reality. Amnon watched Tamar; the fact she was a virgin—pure, and innocent turned him on. Amnon fantasized about being with Tamar in the sickest of ways. Instead of redirecting his thoughts with prayer, meditation, and spiritual consultation, he focused on them repeatedly with each coming day; he had to have her.

Amnon knew very well the sin involved with having such defiling thoughts about his sister, Tamar. Amnon would not dare mention his thoughts to his brothers— and certainly not to King David. He would not tell them he had been fantasizing about his sister, Tamar, to the point he had fallen in love with her and desired an intimate relationship. Amnon was well aware that if he disclosed such thoughts, he would be considered an abomination and would likely be put away. When around his family, he acted normal and was merely affectionate to Tamar as any big brother would be. Because no one knew of Amnon's obsession, he had no support; he had no one to tell him it was okay to be in love with his sister. Thus, Amnon did not act on his sick thoughts.

Very often, the abuser in our life, although we did not know or recognize it, spotted and admired us from afar off. He paid attention to us long before the initial introduction. If not us specifically, he was focused on the idea of having a good person in his life, knowing very well he was undeserving. Perhaps, he was attracted to our innocence and purity. Maybe, it was our love for God that attracted him. An abuser can be so full of hatred and other issues, that he imagines that being in a relationship with a good person will somehow cleanse him of his impurities. Either way, an abuser knows he is not good enough; he knows deep down inside he has unresolved issues which have not only destroyed him, but everyone else who has come into his life—and will eventually cause us a world of pain. Instead of seeking God and asking Him for healing and deliverance, he spots someone who is good and whom he thinks will make him feel better. Next, he develops and perfects a plan to get what he thinks he wants.

As mentioned earlier, up until this time, Amnon had resigned his obsessions to his own imagination and had resisted the urge to act on thoughts of being with his sister; he knew his family members would not support something so awful. Amnon had no one to validate his thoughts until Jonadab came along. Jonadab, Amnon's cousin, was very cunning. He knew how to conjure up and carry out very devious plans. Jonadab was skilled enough to get away with his devious plans without others knowing his involvement. He was very laid back and could almost go unnoticed; he stayed in the background, but still had a lot of influence. Jonadab knew how to manipulate people to get what he wanted; he knew how to 'grease the right palms.' In this case, Amnon was the son of King David. It was beneficial for Jonadab to remain close with him. If Amnon somehow still became the King of Israel, Jonadab could imagine himself being his right hand. Jonadab was the type of man who would whisper in people's ears to start confusion and then sit back to watch the show. He would never fight for himself, and if confronted about his part in the confusion, would likely place blame on someone else. Jonadab did not care about anyone except himself and only befriended a person to see what he could get out of him or her. He stayed connected to a situation just long enough to stay informed and cover himself; he always had an opinion and did not hesitate to whisper his unsolicited advice. In actuality, Jonadab was also an abuser. He carried one of the distinct characteristics of an abuser—manipulation. Jonadab misled people and manipulated events to his own benefit. He did not consider or care who was hurt as a result of his bad advice and careless behavior.

It is very common for an abuser to have fellow abusers and manipulators in his life. There is usually someone in his life that is willing to justify, validate, and celebrate his abusive traits and behaviors. An abuser often has someone in his life that is unwilling to confront his behavior when it is not in line with the Word of God. Jonadab was this type of person in Amnon's life. Amnon went directly to the one person in his life he knew would not challenge his lust. He knew Jonadab would listen and agree with his sick thoughts. As expected, Jonadab responded to Amnon's conversation in a way that offered approval.

Very often, we know in our own minds that we are being emotionally abused, but because there may be one or a few people justifying the abuser's behaviors, we begin to doubt our better judgment. Many of us choose to confide in our abuser's family and friends hoping they will agree with us, give us sound advice, or even talk to our abuser. Consequently, we become disappointed when those people do not stand up for us and further contribute to our abuser's behaviors. We start to think we are the one with the problem and may be over exaggerating. If Tamar had gone to Jonadab in confidence about her attack, he possibly would have told her, "It's not that bad; you are overreacting. He is your brother; no harm done." Jonadab likely would have tried to intimidate and guilt Tamar by telling her that if she told anyone, she would destroy the royal family. Jonadab was an accomplice and could not be trusted to do the right thing. His allegiance was to Amnon and to himself.

There are always going to be people in our life who are unwilling to get involved or stand up for what is right. Very often, when dealing with our abuser's family, they too will be willing to justify the abuser's behavior. Deep down, they know our abuser has issues; they realize if we do not deal with him, they will be the ones having to put up with his issues. In actuality, they are grateful to have him off their hands. As well, just because we have no one in our own circle to validate our hurt feelings, does not mean we are not in an abusive relationship. It is not all the time that our circle is able to look in and see the abuse. This is especially true if our close family members and loved ones are not believers. When we are dealing with unbelievers, they do not have the spiritual discernment to distinguish between right and wrong. It is likely they are currently experiencing or have experienced this same type of turmoil in their own life and consider it normal; but God never intended for us to be abused.

Jonadab, Amnon's cousin, was an accomplice to the attack on Tamar. In essence, Jonadab validated Amnon by making him believe his sexual feelings towards his sister were normal and nothing to be ashamed of. Jonadab provoked Amnon's sense of entitlement in being the King's son. That is, he made Amnon feel entitled to have Tamar. Jonadab said "Why art thou, being the King's son, so lean from day to day? What is wrong with you? You do not look well, Amnon." Thriving from Jonadab's attention and sympathy, Amnon replied, "I am in love with Tamar, my brother Absalom's sister." Jonadab did not stop to question or challenge Amnon's thoughts. Instead, he immediately helped him develop a plan. He advised Amnon to lie down on the bed and make his self seem sick. He gave Amnon ideas such as starving himself and putting makeup on to make his story more convincing. In other words, Jonadab encouraged Amnon to do whatever it took to get what he wanted. Jonadab knew that if Amnon looked sick, the word would get back to King David and he would come to see about his son. Jonadab persuaded Amnon, "You know your father, King David, loves you and would do anything not to lose you. So when your father comes in, let him think you are sick. Convince him that the only thing that will make you feel better is if he allows Tamar to come and feed you."

Together, Jonadab and Amnon developed a very cunning plan. When we consider emotional abuse, we will see that it is rooted in manipulation. To put it another way, the abuser wants us to see, feel, or think something is there that is not. In addition, if we pay attention, we will notice that the abuser is not only manipulating us, but he is likely manipulating someone else in his life to get what he wants. Manipulation is nothing more than a fancy way of saying a lie; it is both a characteristic and product of abuse. That is, emotional abuse involves manipulation and further breeds manipulation. In an emotionally abusive relationship, much like the actions of Amnon, the abuser will pretend to be something he is not and thus create false feelings in us. In other words, we fall head over heels in love with someone who is not who he says he is. The abuser has put his best foot forward. He talks gentle; he brings flowers and tells us what he knows we want to hear. He even pretends to be desolate hoping to invoke the compassion that is deeply embedded in us. After all, he has watched long enough to know what is important to us. He sees our desire to help people, be needed, and be loved.

In this story, there was more than one victim of Amnon's abuse. Amnon also deceived his father, King David, as a tactic to get Tamar. In other words, the emotional abuse started long before it got to Tamar. Amnon followed through with his plan. Amnon made himself feel and look sick. As expected, King David, being a loving father, came to Amnon. He said, "Amnon, why are you sick? What can I do?" As planned, Amnon responded, "I pray thee, let Tamar, my sister, come, and make me a couple of cakes in my sight, that I may eat at her hand." Then King David sent home to Tamar—not even knowing what he was doing to his baby girl. He sent home to his baby Tamar and said, "Go see about your brother. He is asking for you. He is sick and wants to see you." King David did not know what was going to happen. So not only was Amnon about to abuse Tamar, but he was abusing his father, King David.

If King David had recognized the events that were about to occur, he would have been angry, devastated, embarrassed and most important, would have felt humiliated at the idea that his own son was trying to deceive him; King David would have felt manipulated and been enraged. Even after the rape, we can imagine the humiliation King David felt as he realized he was the one who sent his baby girl to Amnon. Although there was no way he could have known what was going to happen, he likely still felt responsible and guilty. Abuse usually leaves us with a sense of guilt. The guilt comes from us knowing we should have done something to stop the abuse. When considering emotional abuse, the aftermath often includes humiliation, guilt, shame, and regret. We repeatedly torture our self with the idea, "If only I had known the type of person he was, I would have made a different decision."

Amnon was not only preparing to abuse his sister Tamar, but the chain of abuse had already affected his father, King David. It is important to pay attention to the fact that Amnon's abuse started before Tamar. How is this relevant? Very often, we feel as if there was something in us, something we did, a fault or lack in us that changed that person to being who they are towards us. We feel as if we somehow caused the abuser to mistreat us. We are convinced the abuser was a good person before we got to him; somehow, something we did made him become an abuser. Satan is a liar; that is not the truth. The story of Tamar is such a great example because it illustrates how Amnon's emotional abuse started long before it got to Tamar. In other words, Amnon had a history of manipulating, lying, and humiliating. The fact is; we did not cause the abuser to abuse us. His abuse was intentional; he abused us because he made the choice to do so. It was not accidental. We did not make the abuser hurt us and nine times out of ten, his abuse started before he got to us.

Tamar journeyed to Amnon's house. When she arrived there, he was lying down and playing sick. Very disheartened to see her eldest brother sick and distressed, Tamar took the flour she had brought with her and kneaded it. After care and preparation, the flour was ready and she made cakes in Amnon's sight. Tamar was doing what she thought she was supposed to do. Like Tamar, many of us find our self in an abusive relationship doing all we can to support the relationship. We are cooking, cleaning, making beds, and raising children. We are doing the work we think we are supposed to do.

Tamar took the pan and poured it out before Amnon. She presented the cake to him to eat, but he refused it. He acted as if something was wrong with him and with Tamar's cakes. At this point, Amnon was playing the part. Everyone started asking him what was wrong. Tamar began to have even more compassion on him. She even considered trying to make the cakes a different way to please her brother. She was desperate to make him happy. Of all the sisters Amnon could have called upon, Amnon wanted to see her and she did not want to disappoint him. After playing the part long enough, Amnon said to the people around, "Have all the men out of here. I want everyone out." Amnon pretended he was so sick that he did not want to eat in front of the other people there, so he sent everyone away—except Tamar.

Amnon's request for everyone to leave seemed innocent enough. After all, Amnon was Tamar's brother. Amnon was also the eldest son, which suggested he was very responsible and would protect his baby sister at all costs. Most importantly, Amnon was King David's son. He would do the right thing. He was supposedly a man of integrity. The fact is, even if someone had accused Amnon of mischief, the people around would mostly have ignored it or would have been afraid to confront Amnon because of his pedigree. "Amnon is not that kind of guy. He has always been a good boy. He has been right there with his father. He is at all of the celebrations with his royal attire on. He even gives to the poor. Amnon could have any woman he wants. Why would he go after his baby sister?" Everyone exited the room without hesitation; they trusted Amnon and so did Tamar.

Finally, it was just Amnon and Tamar in the room. Amnon had isolated Tamar; he got her away from her family and friends. Tamar was isolated from anyone who would have been able to see and question Amnon's actions. She was far away from her maidens and spiritual coverings. She was alone with Satan. In this relationship, her abuser did not want her to be around the people whom she loved, the people who would speak up for her, and the people who would protect her.

Amnon isolated Tamar. On the other hand, although he sent the people out of the room, they were likely still standing around the door and could hear what was going on inside the room. They still had some level of access to Tamar and Amnon. Access to Tamar not only meant that other people could hear Tamar, but also she could hear their voices and opinions. Very importantly, the fact that the people could still access Tamar and Amnon meant that Amnon could still be held accountable; there were still potential witnesses to his sin. Amnon was a coward. Despite the harm he so boldly intended for Tamar, he still very much cared about what other people thought about him. He did not want his name to be tarnished.

It was at this point Amnon decided not only was he going to send the people away, but he also made the decision to get Tamar into the inner chamber. The significance of the inner chamber is that, it was quiet there. The chamber was a room hidden away in the inner parts of Amnon's home. There were no windows or exterior doors, and the chamber was likely sound proof. In the chamber, not only was Tamar away from people, but she was so far inside that no one could hear her scream; no one could hear her reaching out for help. Not only were her loved ones unable to see her, but now they were unable to hear her; she was unreachable. She was alone in a chamber with someone she would soon find out was a monster.

Amnon said to Tamar, "Come into the chamber and feed me your cakes." Very likely, Tamar began to feel a little uncomfortable. She began to wonder why she was asked to come into the chamber without any attendants. This was not customary for the daughter of the King. Still, Tamar rationalized the great assignment given to her and counted it an honor and privilege to tend to such a great man. Tamar still did not know the real Amnon; at this point, no one knew besides Jonadab. It was likely there were others who questioned Amnon's actions—especially now that he had taken Tamar into the inner chamber. "This is not normal, but it is none of my business," they thought to themselves. Tamar too, ignored her intuition and proceeded to do what she was told. Here she is; a virgin—Amnon's sister. Not knowing what was going on, Tamar simply followed her eldest brother's directions.

As Tamar approached Amnon to feed him, he took hold of her and said, "Come lie with me my sister." Suddenly, the monster, Amnon, was revealed. Tamar was shocked and scared. Amnon asked Tamar to do something that he knew was wrong. He said, "Come lie with me." At this point, the abuse became overt. It was no longer hidden or subtle. Amnon did not care anymore—no more precautions for him. Besides, no one else was there to pass judgment or stop him.

Amnon did not simply ask Tamar to sleep with her, but he first grabbed her. Amnon was trying to make a point to Tamar; he wanted to intimidate her. He wanted her to be afraid of him with the hope that she would not put up a fight. Amnon tried to frighten Tamar by showing her he was much stronger than she was. Already, Amnon had exercised authority by making everyone leave them, but now he showed her that he could 'handle' her. The fact that Amnon first asked Tamar to sleep with him was not because he was trying to be nice. His invitation to Tamar was his last attempt to clear his conscious. Amnon knew he was willing to take it as far as he needed to get what he wanted out of Tamar, but he figured he would at least ask just in case Tamar was willing to sin. Amnon was not only obsessed with Tamar, but was also jealous of her purity. Not only was she beautiful and a virgin, but she a representation of the type of person Amnon would never be. She was good and wholesome. She still had something of value.

Tamar had all kinds of thoughts going through her mind. This was her eldest brother, the eldest son of King David. Not only was he her brother, but he was a leader in the kingdom. Should she sleep with him? It would be better than a rape by her brother; after all, she was a virgin. However, sleeping with her brother was an abomination. Not only was it wrong in man's eyes, but Tamar knew that it was wrong in her heavenly Father's eyes.

Finally, Tamar answered Amnon. She said, "Nay my brother, do not force me. This is not right. Of course, I am not going to sleep with you." Everyone was gone and Amnon and Tamar were now so far in the chamber, that no one could hear them. At this point Amnon felt comfortable crossing limits and boundaries with Tamar. However, when he asked her to sleep with him, she boldly replied, "no." With Tamar's rejection, Amnon allowed himself to turn up the heat. That is, he lost all reservation, and the abuse, which he had hidden so well, came from behind the shadows and was visible. In an abusive relationship, the abuse becomes apparent when there is something about our lifestyle that challenges the lust in the abuser. Amnon actually went in hoping Tamar would commit sin with him—expecting to justify his own behavior and make himself feel better. His false hopes kept him from immediately forcing her, but now that hope was gone.

When Tamar rejected Amnon's advances, his physical, sexual, and emotional abuse became apparent. Again, when something about our lifestyle, decisions, and characteristics challenges the lust of the abuser's flesh, the abuse will become visible. The abuse was already there, but it was hidden; it was camouflaged. It was there in the form of manipulation. The hidden abuse came in the form of her abuser telling her the things she wanted to hear—flattery. The abuse was there all along, but Tamar did not recognize it for what it really was. However, when Tamar stood up for what was right, her light began to shine in the midst of darkness. Tamar's stand for holiness caused light to expose Amnon's hidden abuse. When the lust of the flesh is challenged, abuse becomes apparent. It is when Tamar refused to go along with his wrongdoing and decided to stand up for herself that Satan showed himself. Tamar answered Amnon, "No. Amnon, do not force me. No such thing should be done in Israel. I am your sister. Do not do this folly."

Tamar not only responded 'no' to Amnon's sexual advances, but she also called his sin what it was. She said boldly, "This is wrong, this is shame, this is sin, and this is a curse." In her argument, Tamar made Amnon consider her future and the consequences of his actions. She said to him, "And where will I go once you have done this to me? Where will I go once I have had sex with my own brother? What will I do?" Tamar took it even further to make Amnon consider his own future as well. She said to Amnon, "And where will you go? You are the son of the King. You are probably next in line for the throne. Thou shall be as one of the fools in Israel. Now therefore I pray you, speak to the King. He will give you anyone you want." She said to Amnon, "Do it the proper way; go talk to our father about this. Let him know what is going on. See what he says about your actions." Even through all that Tamar had witnessed thus far, she still gave Amnon the opportunity to back out of this horrendous act with no harm done. Tamar was conscious of her own well-being as well as Amnon's soul. Nevertheless, Amnon was too far-gone and Tamar's questions posed a threat to him. His sin had progressed and his pride had now been attacked. The goodness in Tamar challenged Amnon's lust. II Samuel 13:14 reads, *"Howbeit, he would not hearken unto her voice, but being stronger than she, forced her and lay with her."*

When Amnon raped Tamar, he took from her that which was most precious to her. He took the gift she saved for her betrothed. In that society, a woman's virginity kept her separate from the other women. She was deemed pure, valuable, and was set apart. She was the hope and reward for a hard worker who sought to marry and have children with a good woman. No other man, besides her husband, would have been witness to the intimate details of her body and sexuality. Amnon knew the gift Tamar held and thought that by having sex with her, her goodness would somehow pour into him. To be clear, Amnon could have had sex with anyone in the kingdom, but he chose someone who was virtuous hoping he would then share in her same virtue. When Tamar challenged Amnon and refused to partake in sin with him, he went forward with his plan to rape her.

After Amnon raped Tamar, the Bible says he hated her exceedingly. He called in the guards and essentially kicked Tamar out into the streets. How could he hate the woman that he had been so in love and obsessed with just minutes before? Amnon hated Tamar because the goodness that he thought would rub off on him by having sex with her did not. In other words, he did not feel better, and in fact, he hated himself even more than before. Not only did Amnon not feel better, but immediately after raping Tamar, he also felt the overwhelming guilt of what he had just done to her; he raped his own sister. Amnon was burdened with the guilt and fear that someone would find out about what he had done. He was consumed with hatred for himself for committing such a terrible act. Amnon finally had to face the truth of the type of man he was. He knew very well that what he had done was wrong and that he had hurt Tamar. Amnon became angry because he knew there was no way to fix or reverse the damage he had done; therefore, he hated Tamar. Tamar was now living proof of the evil that was inside of him. After raping Tamar, Amnon had not been changed. He was still the very ugly person that he was before. Amnon was angry with Tamar for not being able to change him. Therefore, he humiliated her further by calling in the guards and kicking her out of his house as if she had done something wrong.

The story goes on to say that Tamar was forced out of Amnon's house and was forever changed. There, right on the street outside of Amnon's home, Tamar, being overwhelmed with grief, ripped her clothes and pulled her hair out of her head. She could not believe it; she wanted to die. Tamar remained alone and lived in her brother Absalom's home for the rest of her life. How sad it must have been for Tamar to have never married or birthed a child because of this tragic event.

Undoubtedly, Tamar's physical scars healed, but her spirit was forever wounded. *"The spirit of a man will sustain his infirmity, but a wounded spirit who can bear"* (Prov. 18:14)?

Chapter XI

I AM TAMAR

I am Tamar. You are Tamar. Almost anyone who has ever been in an abusive relationship can relate to some aspect of Tamar's tragedy. Perhaps we were an innocent virgin, who fell in love with and eventually married an abuser, or someone who was supposed to protect us sexually abused us. Either way, we all can relate to Tamar's story in some way. We all ask the question, "Why?" The answer is, Satan looked at us and saw we were going to make an impact on the kingdom of God. He knew he could not use just any tactic against us, so he crept in and attacked us in a way that would leave long-term damage to our spirit. He directly aimed at affecting our ability to walk in the Spirit and produce the fruit of the Spirit. Satan was determined to destroy us. Nevertheless, *"He which hath begun a good work in you shall perform it"* (Phil. 1:6). Satan really should have killed us. Now we are back and more powerful than ever. What Satan meant for bad, God turned around and made it work out for our good.

Infatuation

Consider Tamar, a virgin child, who felt honored and privileged to be favored by her eldest brother, Amnon. Even for us today, what an honor it is for someone to show us attention and tell us we are beautiful or handsome. What an honor it is for someone to want to be our friend and be in our interpersonal life. For many of us, we go into the relationship innocently—not realizing at all the danger we are walking into, and ignoring any red flags. Things are seemingly falling into place and we assume we are very much in love. When we initially meet an abuser, we do not know he is an abuser. We do not realize that the lover we become infatuated with is eventually going to torment our spirit. When we meet our abuser, he puts his best foot forward. We cannot see the hidden neglect, humiliation, and degradation that will soon come to the forefront of his character. We are not being called stupid and criticized for merely being our self in the beginning. In the beginning, he is smiling in our face and flattering us with what he knows we want to hear. It is not hard to guess; we all want to be loved. In the story of Tamar, she likely said to herself, "I am the baby sister. Amnon, my big brother, is asking for me; I feel honored." Amnon was saying things about Tamar that made her feel wanted and needed; he made her feel special. It was very easy for Tamar to become vulnerable because perhaps she had no one else in her life offering her that type of attention at the time. Not only that, but Amnon also sent messages through other people to make everyone think he sincerely cared for and admired his little sister Tamar. He said, "No one can make these cakes like my sister Tamar." We can imagine people in the community saying, "Wow, they really have a great relationship."

Much like Tamar, many of us find our self doing what our abuser wants us to do, and what we assume we are supposed to be doing. We are not forced, but in actuality, we feel honored to be in companionship with this person. For Tamar, it was not just anyone who sent for her to tend to Amnon—it was King David. Tamar felt honored, privileged, and special to get such great attention. All of her friends and family members knew about her special assignment. Very often, we become 'caught up' in the attention of our relationship without paying attention to the personality and characteristics of the person we are with; we ignore the details. So here, Tamar was in the chamber, doing what she thought she was supposed to do.

Playing Dress-Up

Walk in the Spirit, so you will not fulfill the lust of the flesh (Gal. 5:16). Considering Amnon, he manipulated the environment to get to Tamar. He said, "Your cakes are delicious. Only my little sister can make me feel better." When we have purpose, Satan will directly play on our weakness. For many of us, our area of vulnerability is our desperation to be in a relationship. Remember, our desire for a relationship is NOT a weakness; God designed us this way. The weakness comes in when we become desperate for a relationship and willing to do anything to get it. We were reared to be wives and mothers. We played with Barbie dolls. We played dress-up with our parents' shoes, wigs, make-up, and aprons; we were reared to fulfill such roles. We deeply desire to be loved and to bestow love. When we finally get the chance to be in a relationship, we fall right back into our childhood roll without considering the details of our adult relationship. We have to be careful to seek God in everything we do so that we do not fall prey to a relationship that is not of God.

Desperation Leads to Frustration

Reflecting on our life, we can all admit that at some point, we were so desperate to be in a relationship that against our better judgment, we ended up with an abuser. We wanted to be in a relationship so bad that we were willing to settle for anything. Anyone who has ever been in an abusive relationship can admit there were signs along the way indicating the relationship was not right, but we ignored them. Something did not coincide with our spirit, but we wanted so badly to be in a relationship, and ignored our good conscious. Perhaps, we had never had a boyfriend before and he was the first one. Perhaps we were fearful that we would not find anyone else. Maybe, we were walking after the lust of our flesh and wanted to have sex, so we ignored all of the signs. We ignored the counsel from our family, friends, and even our pastor; we decided we were going to do what we wanted to do. If we can be honest, we saw signs within our abuser's family and past relationships that told us he was not right for us. We never really understood why his ex broke up with him; the stories he told did not make sense. God always gives us signs that something is not right, but it is up to us to listen. Very often, our own pride gets in the way. We start to think that we do not have to listen to warning from the people in our life. We think we are better than they are; we think we are above God's commandments. Warning always comes before destruction and *"pride goeth before a fall"* (Proverbs 16:18). If we could ask Tamar, she would probably admit that she wondered why, out of everyone Amnon could have called, he called for a little girl to come bake the cakes. She wondered why Amnon sent everyone away and then still took her into the chamber. She was not even that great of a cook.

Hearing God's Voice

God always provides us with a way of escape. Every so often, the way of the escape comes in the form of an initial breakup before we get too deep into the relationship. On the other hand, God may speak to us in the still of the night with direction to leave. However, for fear of being alone, we accept the abuser back into our life. When we do not listen to the voice of God, we are at risk of falling too deeply into an unhealthy relationship. At the end of the day, we cannot put all the blame on the abuser. We have to look at our self as well. When did we get out of line? Had we been walking in the Spirit, we would not have been in the relationship in the first place. However, our flesh became weak; we were so desperate and did not believe the Word of God. *"For my grace is sufficient for you, and my strength is made perfect in weakness. For when I am weak, then I am strong"* (2 Cor. 12:9-10).

Unleashing the Dragon

It is when we are well into the abusive relationship that the abuser will finally show who he really is. When we first get into the relationship, the abuser puts on his best face because he needs to secure our commitment to him. He knows that once we are in the relationship, we will be committed no matter what. However, after the abuser has manipulated us and secured our commitment to him, he becomes too comfortable and begins to make mistakes. The abuser knows he has our heart and instead of nurturing and growing the relationship, he becomes careless. As a result, we begin to notice certain behaviors that do not make sense; we start to notice the carelessness in how he talks to us, his lack of affection, and concern. We begin to question if he has our best interest at heart.

Once the abuser figures out that we are aware of his hostile personality, he becomes fearful and attempts to regain control over us. The abuser becomes fearful of losing a good thing in his life. He senses that we are aware of the evil inside of him and fears we may expose him for who he really is. The abuser knows that our presence in his life is keeping him sane and making him look good. He fears that if we leave him, chaos will enter into his life in a very real way. It seems ironic; although the abuser is hurting the one person who sincerely loves him, he does not want us to leave because he knows the image he is trying to portray to the outside world will become flawed. Especially if the abuser was in a questionable relationship before us, he will be unable to create the same blameless story again. The abuser knows that, if we gather the strength to leave the relationship, the people in his life will figure out that he is, in fact, an abuser.

Conversely, when we stay in the abusive relationship, the abuser is forced to face the reality of who he really is; he is forced to face his demons. He recalls all of his issues from the past; i.e., the people who have hurt him, the people he has hurt, etc. Our light exposes all of his secret issues, and as a result, he hates himself and us. The abuser turns up the heat in the relationship; he tries to do everything he can to hurt us and make our life as miserable as his is. He attempts to destroy our spirit. He wants to kill our character so that he is not the only 'bad' person in the relationship. He wants to create hatred, wrath, envy and other lust of the flesh in us. When something about our personality, character, faith, and strength challenges the lust in the abuser, his abuse will become apparent. The abuser will make our life a living hell. When Tamar challenged Amnon's

103

lust, he attacked her. Up until that time, Tamar was doing everything Amnon wanted her to do. Everything was coming along smoothly and according to Amnon's plan. His manipulation, tricks, and lying had worked. He had manipulated King David, and had even coerced Tamar into the chamber. Now, Tamar was making him cakes like a nice little girl. However, Amnon became careless and invited Tamar to sin. When Tamar called Amnon out on his actions, he attacked her.

Manipulating Our Abuser

When we are in an emotionally abusive relationship, we are constantly focused on our self, what we can do to make the relationship better, and what we can do to make our abuser stop humiliating us. We just want love and we are willing to do anything to get it. This type of fixation is normal; after all, we are hurting. However, this path can very quickly get out of control and can even become destructive. Because we are constantly brainstorming and experimenting with ideas of how to make things better, we end up becoming a manipulator our self. We try to trick and manipulate our abuser into loving us—not realizing that love has to be a free will offering. We are not focused on God and less likely to follow direction from the Holy Spirit. When we recognize our tactics are not working, we become upset and begin to harbor anger and un-forgiveness. We become tormented in our thoughts and soon develop hatred for our abuser. We lose sleep; we become depressed and unable to carry on with our normal routine of life. We become unstable and unpredictable. At this point, Satan has crept in and is now not only using our abuser, but he is using us as well.

Losing Control

When we get out of the will of God, we find our self walking after the lust of the flesh. Let us be clear; lust is more than sex and sexual activities. Satan has fooled us to believe the lust of the flesh only involves sexual sin so that we get out of control in other areas. The lust of the flesh refers to all of the longings of the flesh. Take for example, a moment of rage. Mothers can relate to this; when someone bothers our children, something mysterious happens to our body and its rhythm. Before we know it, the hairs are standing up on our arms and we are ready and willing to fight. Thinking back, we can attest that we instantly felt the strength and desire of the flesh. That quickly, rather than letting the Holy Spirit keep us calm, we moved out of the Spirit and were fulfilling the lust of the flesh. In a relationship, although our spirit hurts from the emotional abuse, our flesh actually feeds on the conflict. This is what Satan wants for our life and that is why he often deceives us through emotionally abusive relationships. Satan wants hatred and wrath; he wants us to walk in envy, jealously, self-hatred, and powerlessness, all which are products of an emotionally abusive relationship and lust of the flesh. Satan wants us to be out of control. Most importantly, Satan wants us to fall into sin and lose our souls. Do not be mistaken—the real danger of being in an emotionally abusive relationship is that we are at risk of losing our souls to sin.

Hell on Earth

In these last and evil days, emotional abuse is one of the primary weapons of Satan because it directly destroys our spirit. If we can rid our self of the affects of emotional abuse, we can find our self starting to walk in the Spirit again, and not the lust of the flesh. *"Now the works of the flesh are made manifest, which are these; adultery, fornication, uncleanness, lasciviousness, idolatry, witchcraft, hatred, variance, emulations, wrath, strife, seditions, heresies, envying, murders, drunkenness, revellings, and such like: of the which I tell you before, as I have told you in time past, that they which do such things shall not inherit the kingdom of God"* (Gal. 5:19-21). We can add to that, not only will those who live like that will not inherit the kingdom of God, but will also be miserable here on earth. We should not want to live hell here on earth, and then die and go to hell, too. It is so important that we walk in the Spirit so we can produce the fruit of the Spirit, which is *"love, joy, peace, longsuffering, gentleness, goodness, faith, meekness, and temperance"* (Gal. 5:22-23).

Background Check

When we go into a new romantic relationship, we become so overjoyed with actually being in a relationship that we do not take the time to do a background check on our new partner. That is, we do not take the time to talk to his friends, or the people who were previously in his life such as his ex-girlfriends or family members. It is important to know if the people in his past and his present respect him as a man. Despite what went wrong in the relationship, basic respect means a lot. We cannot change the past, however, we can learn from the mistakes of the past. When we get into another relationship, we have to be determined to do things differently. We have to compare any new person with the Word of God to find out who he really is. We need to know if he is walking in the Spirit and producing the fruit of the Spirit or if he is fulfilling the lust of the flesh. It is important that we observe and talk to his family, friends, and coworkers. We need to find out if this person, in his past, has produced the fruit of the Spirit. If he has been walking in the lust of the flesh, he is no good for us. After everything we have been through, if we get out of line and fall into another abusive relationship, we are going to be crazy. It is imperative that we walk in the Spirit. We also have to be equally yoked with someone who is walking in the Spirit and producing the fruit of the Spirit in both his life and in ours.

Self-Awareness

We so often overlook emotional abuse because it can be subtle. That is, emotional abuse can be so very unnoticeable that we do not even recognize what is going on.

107

All we know is that something is wrong and we are feeling a certain type of way. We are not able to put our finger on it, or say exactly what it is, but we feel uncomfortable. The sole purpose of emotional abuse is to destroy our spirit so that we will be unable to produce the fruit of the Spirit. We have to take the time to be aware and monitor the condition of our spirit. It is important that we pay attention to our mood, thinking patterns, and behaviors to make sure we are producing the fruit of the Spirit, which is *"love, joy, peace, longsuffering, gentleness, goodness, faith, meekness, and temperance"* (Gal. 5:22-23). There is no law against walking in the Spirit. When we walk in the Spirit, we are not only happy, but we also make those around us feel safe and secure. On the other hand, when we consider the lust of the flesh; there are laws against such things. They hurt people; they cause anger, wrath, violence, and sin.

Righting a Wrong

They say hindsight is 20/20. Through all of the red flags and warnings, somehow we still found our self in an emotionally abusive relationship. If you are currently in an emotionally abusive relationship where suddenly the person you cared for and loved so dearly has become your abuser, there are important steps you must follow. First, go to God in prayer. If your relationship was not founded in truth and holiness, then it was not right in the first place. If you previously had a relationship with God, but did not listen to His voice, then the relationship was out of His will. Pray and ask God for forgiveness. Say, "Lord, I am sorry I disobeyed you. Please, forgive me for my transgressions. Forgive me for being caught up in the lust of my flesh. Forgive me Father for not listening to your Holy Spirit." Believe the prayer you are praying—God is able to fix what is wrong. Next, read Galatians 5:19-23; after you have studied and meditated on the Word of God, look in the mirror and ask yourself, "In my relationship right now, am I able to walk in the Spirit and produce the fruit of the Spirit, or am I walking after the lust of the flesh?" If your relationship has been causing you to walk in the lust of the flesh, then with the help of God, you need to consider making serious changes.

The Original Plan

It was God's original purpose and plan for us to walk in the Spirit. Nevertheless, very often, we find our self rejecting the gift of salvation and walking in the lust of the flesh. The lust of the flesh includes more than just sexual impurities. The lust of the flesh can include hatred, un-forgiveness, envy, jealousy, wrath, fits of rage, and much more. Our flesh wants those things; it is hungry for those things. In the book of Genesis, the story goes that Adam and Eve committed the original sin and ate the apple. It was at that point their flesh became more powerful than their spirit was. Over the generations, man attempted to reconcile his life back to God through sacrifice, but always fell short to sin and the lust of the flesh. That is when God sent the ultimate sacrifice, Jesus. He came and paid for all of the sins humankind had committed, and now we are able to walk in the Spirit again. All we have to do is accept Christ's gift of salvation. *"The word is nigh thee, even in thy mouth, and in thy heart: that is, the word of faith, which we preach; That if thou shalt confess with thy mouth the Lord Jesus, and shalt believe in thine heart that God hath raised him from the dead, thou shalt be saved"* (Rom. 10:8-9).

Chapter XII

RECOVERING FROM ABUSE

Recovery from abuse is a complex process. If not completed properly, it can lead many of us down a very destructive path. The truth is most abusers were once victims of some form of abuse. The difference between a victim and an abuser is merely a lack of healing. That is, when a victim has not been healed from the abuse of his past, he continues to feel out of control. In his attempt to regain control, he finds himself abusing others. Said another way, soon after a victim has suffered abuse of any kind, his immediate mission is to gain back the control and power he lost at the hands of his abuser. He does not want to feel powerless any longer. If a victim is not healed after an abusive relationship, it is human nature and the lust of the flesh for him to attempt to regain control in an unhealthy way. Remember, the lust of the flesh include *adultery, fornication, uncleanness, lasciviousness, idolatry, witchcraft, hatred, variance, emulations, wrath, strife, seditions, heresies, envy, murders, drunkenness,*

revellings, and things like that (Gal. 5:19-21). When a victim has been hurt so badly, to where he is unable to walk in the Spirit and produce the fruit of the Spirit, he will turn to the lust of the flesh and thus find himself appeasing the flesh. The flesh always wants to be in control.

When it comes to abuse, proper recovery really means repairing the spirit. Repairing the spirit must be a slow, well thought out, sensitive and careful process. This process requires time, counseling, biblical teaching and a strong support system in place. However, for many of us, these necessities are either not readily available to us, or we do not take advantage of them because of lack of knowledge or lack of patience. For fear of the abuse repeating itself, we become desperate to regain control. We begin to lash out at family members, children, co-workers, spiritual leaders, and even strangers. We attempt to regain control by taking control from someone else. That is, we find our self taking desperate measures to regain control of our own life by controlling every inch and detail of someone else's life. We are scared to acknowledge that we are broken, extremely damaged, and in need of an emotional and spiritual healing. We are determined that no one is going to know how fragile we are and that we secretly blame our own self for what happened to us.

There is a common saying that "birds of a feather flock together." They say, "An abuser can walk into a room full of people and point out a victim of abuse almost as if he can smell her victim mentality." Many of us can

testify that we come from a long history of abusive relationships; we were bullied in school, or we had abusive
parents, etc. The fact is, after an abusive relationship,
many of us almost immediately fall into another abusive
relationship. This is true, in part, because the abuse is
familiar to us; we are used to and comfortable with it.

Our reasoning for jumping immediately into another
relationship could be our fear of being alone, or we want
to prove to our abuser that we can be with someone
else too. Either way, going into another abusive relationship immediately after already being abused further
damages our spirit. The inevitable failure of the new
relationship will place more guilt and shame on us.
Even if our new partner is not an abuser, the fact is, we
are not healed from the abuse of the past. We are simply
not ready to give all of our self to a new relationship.
The new partner may not understand our struggle. As
time passes, the new partner is unable to handle our
emotional roller coasters and he leaves. This is especially true if sexual intimacy becomes a factor too soon
in the relationship. When sexual intimacy becomes a
factor too soon, we create a new soul tie. Then, without
really paying attention, we start transferring our issues
onto the new partner. As well, if the new partner is an
unbeliever, we are now unequally yoked—again. It is
likely our new partner is not emotionally invested and
may only be interested in the sexual thrills from the
vulnerable, easy-to-get, and recycled victim that we
have become. When the new relationship ends, we are
left with new emotional baggage on top of old abuse.

Time is on Our Side

It is important that, after suffering from emotional abuse, we take the time to properly recover. As mentioned previously, time, a strong support system, counseling, and biblical teaching are crucial in the recovery process. Older people often say, "Time heals all wounds." The role of time in recovery is irreplaceable. Time allows the memories and the feelings associated with the horrific experiences to fade slowly away.

Immediately after a physical injury, the wound is open and exposed; it is vulnerable to germs and sensitive to touch. The wound is pink; if left uncovered, everyone can see our raw flesh. Depending on the type of wound, the doctor will advise us to get rest, avoid pressure on the wound, and keep it covered. Over time, the blood dries up, the tissue begins to thicken, and eventually a scab will form over what used to be an open wound. A similar process is true with regard to recovery from abusive relationships. Immediately after the abuse, or breakup of the relationship, our emotional wounds are open and the pain is overwhelming. Our feelings, weaknesses, and vulnerabilities are out in the open for everyone to see. Our personal matters have been exposed to the public and everyone wants to know the details of what happened. If we allow proper time for healing, the immediate pain of the abuse decreases, we begin to gain back our strength, and eventually we are able to start living somewhat normal life again.

However, much like a physical wound, we still have to be careful even after time has passed. Just because the scab has formed does not mean we are fully recovered. If we pick the scab too soon, the flesh becomes exposed, we are again vulnerable to germs, and the wound may start to bleed all over again. Just because time has passed, does not mean we have fully recovered.

Support System

In addition to time, we need a strong support system. We have to be very careful when choosing a support system after an abusive relationship. As victims of abuse, our favorite loved ones may not be suitable to be a part of our support system. Even if they have experienced abuse in their past, they may not recall the immediate effects and damages to their spirit caused by the abuse. They may lack the necessary sensitivity that we need. These individuals may advise us to 'get over it. "That happened years ago, get over it." However, they just do not understand where we are in that moment. How can they understand? In recovering from abuse, we must have people in our life who understand the dynamics of our brokenness. The fact that someone is a longtime acquaintance or has been through the same thing we have been through does not make him or her the ideal person to be part of our support system.

Our support system must first be a group of believers. These specially selected individuals must be prayer warriors. That is, they must be able to see into our spirit and discern our level of spiritual warfare. Members of our support team are going to be there for us emotionally and spiritually. They are people we can cry to and be honest with, without judgment. At the same time, they are not always going to pat us on the back. There is going to come a time when they will have to tell us to 'suck it up.' Our support system is going to push us to get out of bed when we do not feel like it—even if they have to throw a bucket of water over our head. Our support system will be there to hide our cell phone when, in a moment of desperation, we want to call our abuser because of sexual arousal or loneliness. They are still there for us when we become petty, abusive, or when our crying becomes irritating. Most importantly, they will always tell us the truth no matter what. The truth does not always feel good, but it is always good for us. In recovering from an abusive relationship, it is imperative to have a strong, spirit-filled, support system. Our support system will never leave our side.

Professional Counseling

Mental illness is a condition that inhibits a person's ability to think clearly or rationally about themselves and the world around them. Mental illness is a malfunction of our spirit. Because of mental illness, we are unable to process in a normal capacity; our ability to go about a normal routine as a productive citizen is altered. If something is interfering with our peace of mind and we are unable to live productively, then there is an indication that our ability to walk in the Spirit has been affected. This is not what God wants for us; He wants us to walk in the Spirit, so we can produce the fruit of the Spirit. *"Beloved, I wish above all things that thou mayest prosper and be in health, even as thy soul prospereth"* (3 John 1:2).

In addition to time and a strong support system, it is imperative to see a professional counselor during recovery from abuse. Professional counseling can be completed individually or in a group. Emotional abuse and the ending to a relationship has the ability to attack our psyche. Because of a broken love relationship, many of us can even become suicidal or homicidal. We are human; there is always the chance that we can step outside of reality and become psychotic because of hurt. No one is exempt from suffering a mental health crisis. After we have suffered emotional abuse, we feel worthless as if we deserved the abuse or brought it on our self. It is important to have a professional counselor in our life to point out the irrational thoughts that linger from emotional abuse.

Take for example Kristen, who met Darren when she was 15 years old. She became pregnant at 16 and they were married at 18 years old when she was pregnant with their second child. She never finished high school and was a full time homemaker for the majority of the past 20 years. Darren finished high school and secured a job at the local construction company. As time passed, he moved up in the company and made a great living for his family. They went to church every Sunday and they both sang on the choir. Over the years, although he admits Kristen was a great mother to their four children, he became irritated by her dependency on him. It felt to Darren that Kristen could not do anything on her own. Every time he turned around, she was asking him for his hard-earned money. Not to mention, he was somewhat embarrassed to take his high school dropout wife to his job events. While all his colleagues were showing off their lawyer and doctor wives, he shushed his own wife who could barely read.

Darren had forgotten the many times Kristen wanted to go back to school and get a job, but he refused to pay for daycare. There was one time Kristen got a job and started bringing home a decent amount of money; Kristen asked Darren to help around the home and perhaps help the kids with their homework. Darren refused; he still expected Kristen to carry out all of the household duties. Kristen became overwhelmed and eventually quit her job.

Twenty years into the marriage, Darren became increasingly irritated with Kristen who was so desperately trying to make him happy. Darren frequently called Kristen names, compared her to the wives of his colleagues, and made her feel worthless. One day, Darren decided he had enough and ended the marriage. He became so verbally and emotionally abusive to Kristen that she had no choice but to leave their home and live with her sister. After a few weeks of living with her sister, Kristen was expected to get a job, but had difficulty finding a job without a high school diploma. She asked her husband for money, but he refused. Darren, who felt he was better off without his wife, continued to go to the church. Kristen, however, was embarrassed for everyone to know her business and no longer attended the church. Kristen started to feel like a burden on her family and she had no one to talk to about it. She fell into a deep depression and used medications to drown out the pain. She had no money and was practically homeless, except for her sister's couch.

One day, Kristen met an old high school classmate in the store and he invited her to dinner. At dinner, Kristen quickly disclosed to him everything that had been going on in her life. He told her he understood and invited her to his house to talk more. He told her all the right things and she admitted she just wanted to be held. Kristen, who had not had sex in several months and had never had sex with anyone besides Darren, became vulnerable, and had sex with the new man. After a few days, she was excited to tell her sister about the wonderful and sensitive person she had reunited with. While speaking with her sister, Kristen was devastated to find out that she slept with a married man. When she called to confront him, he confirmed his marriage and made it clear to Kristen that he wanted nothing to do with her.

Something snapped in Kristen. She could not believe it! It was at that point Kristen decided she could no longer trust anyone; everyone was against her. Her husband of 20 years had betrayed her, and in her mind, she believed her sister really wanted her to leave, too. She also believed the church and community members were gossiping about her. Kristen became extremely overwhelmed in her thoughts of distrust; she was unable to distinguish between what was real and imagined. It became difficult for Kristen to sleep and eat. She became so angry; she could barely hold down conversations without becoming paranoid and accusing people of being against her. Kristen's thoughts developed into delusions. All of a sudden, Kristen started to believe her sister was trying to poison her and she refused to eat. She also refused to take baths or seek medical attention. After losing almost 100 pounds from not eating, her family members called for help and Kristen was hospitalized.

Kristen's story may seem a little farfetched, but scenarios like this occur everyday. No one is exempt from something like this happening. Kristen's life was turned upside down, and worst of all her spirit was broken. Marriage is the only subject in the Bible for which two spirits are joined; and thus in divorce, our one spirit becomes broken, severed, and in disarray. A reader may be thinking, "Well, I've been with my life partner for 20 years; that is just like a marriage." Although there is longevity there, and you possibly lived as if you were married, the fact is your two spirits were never joined under God; it is just different. Nevertheless, a breakup or a divorce is a major life change, and should not be taken for granted.

No one is exempt from experiencing a mental health crisis. Someone once said, "Almost 99% of mental health crises can be traced to some element of grief/

loss" (Brady, 2012). Very often, when we consider loss, we specifically reference loss of life. However, loss can come in various forms, i.e., loss of a job, loss of mobility, fewer supports, loss of an idea, etc. This 'universal loss theory' is applicable to love and relationships. Many of us have suffered loss of a romantic relationship, loss of the idea of what love should have been like, or loss of hope because we feel we should have been married by now. Many young people have high levels of anxiety waiting for love to come. We suffer with mental anguish and disappointment of not having love in our life. If we are not careful, mild moments of despair can turn into a mental health crisis. For example, it is very easy to despair about our love life to the point that we are unable to get out of bed in the morning or take care of our children. It becomes harder for us to bounce back because of the element of loss in our life.

Although many friends and acquaintances will encourage us to get over the broken relationship right away, if they have not suffered through a divorce, they may not be acquainted with our feelings of grief. In actuality, part of our self has just died. When we lose a loved one, we need the support of family members and even a grief counselor. The same is urgently true for a divorce or separation. A divorce is often compared to a death. The Bible discusses a marriage, abusive or not as this, *"For this cause shall a man leave his mother and father, and cleave unto his wife; and the two shall be one flesh: so they are no more two, but one flesh. What therefore God hath joined together, let not man put asunder"* (Matt. 19:5-6). When

121

that relationship is broken, a person must grieve not only the loss of the relationship but part of themselves as well.

Grief looks different for different people. Some people avoid grieving for years by jumping immediately into another long-term relationship. It is so important to realize we are human and we need help. Pastors are very useful in divorce and separation as they are able to discern our level of warfare. Sometimes, we can get so weak in our spirit that we cannot pray. Pastors are able to intercede for us; they renounce Satan's plan to kill our spirit. Professional counselors are helpful because they can point out to us the irrational thoughts we have. Very importantly, unlike the support system, which may consist of family members and close friends, the counselor remains appropriately detached from our personal life so they can identify warning signs of suicidal or homicidal thoughts and behaviors. If necessary, the counselor is able to take the necessary precautions to keep us safe and refer to a psychiatrist for medication, if necessary. We believe in God, but if our spirit is so desperately broken, we are not able to exercise our faith in God. The flesh may be overpowering our spirit and creating chaos in our mind. Until we are able to walk productively in the Spirit and produce the fruit of the Spirit, it is wise to seek professional help.

Biblical Teaching

Of all the recovery methods discussed, the most important is biblical teaching. It is imperative that we go to the Word of God on a daily basis through personal Bible study, prayer, and meditation. With any issue in life, especially issues of the heart, we can go directly to the Word of God to find example and direction. It is equally important we go to a Bible believing church for spiritual guidance and be around the people of God. Many of us are inclined to stay home from church during tough times. This is particularly true when going through emotional pain; we tend to isolate our self. This is a trick of Satan to destroy our spirit even more. In addition, many of us also stay home from church because we feel we do not need it; we believe we can effectively study the Bible at home or watch church on television. However, the vast importance of going to church is because God is there. In the book of II Chronicles, God gave King Solomon very specific instructions on how to build the temple. After it was completed, God said to King Solomon, *"Now my eyes and my ears will be especially attent to the prayers offered in this place"* (2 Chron. 7:15). God is there at the temple to listen to and answer our prayers. In addition, there is strength among the people of God. In the House of God, we are able to hear the testimony of people who have also been through traumatic events. As well, we are able to solicit the prayers of the saints for spiritual strength. Through worship service, pastoral sermons, Bible Study and participation in the ministries of the church, the pastor and leaders are able to teach and help us learn to walk in the Spirit again and produce the fruit of the Spirit. *"Do not forget to assemble yourselves together often with the saints"* (Heb. 10:25).

123

Forgiveness

One of the benefits of biblical teaching is that it instructs us on the principle of forgiveness. *"Forgive us our debts as we forgive our debtors"* (Matt. 6:12). This step in recovery from emotional abuse is crucial. We cannot recover from emotional abuse if we do not forgive those who have hurt us. Forgiveness is not for the person who hurt and betrayed us—forgiveness is for our own benefit. When we have not forgiven the person who has hurt us, we give him power. The sad part is that our abuser may not even know he still has this power over us. Every time we even think about the hurt, we become sad and overwhelmed with grief. Our entire day can become unproductive; and we isolate our self—all because of a memory of something that happened in the past. It is almost as if we have pushed the repeat button; our moments of hurt and despair are on rewind. Furthermore, un-forgiveness makes us angry and hard to deal with. We become cruel to anyone who reminds us of our abuser and we find our self alone and bitter.

Again, forgiveness is not for the abuser; forgiveness is for the recovery of the victim. Forgiveness releases the power of the emotional abuse from over our life. Without forgiveness, the abuser will continue to have power over us. Long after the abuse is over, the abuser is able to control us much as if we are a puppet on a string. Ironically, the abuser has no idea of their continued power over us. Forgiveness is two-fold. First, we must forgive our self. Why do we need forgiveness if we are not the ones who inflicted the pain? When we point one finger at someone, the rest of our fingers point back at us. In analyzing an abusive relationship, we must examine our own sin in the relationship. We were not completely innocent. If we can admit, we disobeyed the voice of God when we got into the relationship in the first place. More than likely, at some point in the beginning of the relationship, we began to walk less in the Spirit and slowly began to fulfill the lust of the flesh. Second, after we have forgiven our self, then we can forgive our abuser. God told the accusers of Mary Magdalene, *"He who is without sin cast the first stone"* (John 8:7). We all deserve forgiveness; if you do not believe that, then go back to #1. Jesus died for all of us; our abuser has a soul too. Our prayer should be that God would forgive them, and change their life around so that He will get the glory out of their life too. This should be especially true if children are involved. How glorious for children to have two saved parents.

Many of us try to forgive, but are unsuccessful. No matter what we do, we find our self thinking and focused on the hurt of the past. Sitting at work, at the gym, in the park, and even at church, we are tormented with thoughts of hurt. We try to psych our self out and redirect our thoughts so we do not think about the emotional abuse. We pray repeatedly, asking God to help us to forgive, but nothing seems to work; we are still tormented. Although there may be many suggestions on how to forgive, there is only one surefire way to forgive someone who has hurt us. *"Forgetting those things which*

125

are behind, I press towards the mark of the high calling which is in Christ Jesus" (Phil. 3:13-14). The benefit of hurt is that it gives us the incredible opportunity to look to God from which our help comes from. Sometimes, it is not until we face hurt and emotional pain that we take the time to get to know God. That is why He allows us to go through trying times—so that He can get our attention. True forgiveness occurs when we start to pursue our purpose in God. It really is common sense. When we pursue our purpose, we take focus off our problems. We eventually forget about the hurt because we are now occupied with pursuing Christ. True happiness is only yielded when we pursue our calling in Christ.

If you find yourself struggling with forgiveness, it is important that you seek God immediately. If you do not know what your purpose is, then ask God. Start with volunteering in your church or community. There are plenty orphans, seniors, and disadvantaged citizens who would appreciate a visit or conversation from you. The fact is; your situation could be worse. Go down to the domestic violence shelter, hospital, or even the city morgue, and listen to or read other people's stories. Keep yourself busy pursuing something besides yourself, and over time, you will find yourself fulfilled in a way you have never experienced before.

Self-Care

A final step in recovering from abuse is to love our self. That is, we should not only take care of the spiritual and mental parts of us, but we must also take care and pamper our natural bodies. *"What? know ye not that your body is the temple of the Holy Ghost which is in you, which ye have of God, and ye are not your own"* (1 Cor. 6:19). Self-care can be accomplished through daily exercise and a healthy diet. Daily exercise allows a healthy amount of dopamine to flow, which in turn helps to increase our positive moods. High levels of carbohydrates tend to slow us down and decrease our energy levels. As well, pampering our self through regular hair appointments and trips to the spa not only make us look better, but also allow us to feel better. Our body is a temple, and we must take care of and nurture it, especially in times of distress.

Chapter VIII

CHILDREN AND ABUSE

I n discussion of emotional abuse, we want to be clear and say children are powerless. Children cannot defend themselves from abuse and they are unable to process the damage that abuse has on their spirit. They have neither the emotional nor the physical strength to overpower their abuser. For the most part, children do not know they are being abused unless they are taught by parents or community leaders. Their adult parents and community leaders are mandated to protect them from predators. Unfortunately, for children, their abusers are often the very people who are supposed to protect them. Looking back at the story of Tamar, she was only a child. There were several adults who should have and could have protected her, but they merely overlooked all of the signs. We must step up and protect our children.

Parents frequently overlook the vast forms of abuse and often fail to recognize the severe impact which abuse has on the spirit and functioning of our children.

The affects of abuse are apparent not just throughout their childhood, but well into their adult life. When addressing abuse, we should extend our focus beyond the immediate wounds of physical or sexual abuse, especially as it relates to children. There is no doubt that physical and sexual abuses are devastating events, but physical wounds do mend after a time. It is the emotional damage, which lingers on long after the physical wounds heal; the damage to their spirit is what actually causes problems later on down the road. The affects of emotional abuse last long after the child is grown and out of the house. Damage to the spirit creates the lasting scars.

As parents, most of us cannot imagine killing our children's spirit, but we do it regularly by the decisions we make. There is danger in remaining in an unequally yoked and unhealthy relationship when children are involved. We do much more damage to our children by exposing them to an abusive relationship. No one wants to be a single parent and God understands that, but He also holds us accountable for the well-being of our children.

It is important that parents, especially those that claim to be believers, *"train up a child in the way he should go: and when he is old, he will not depart from it"* (Prov. 22:6). This passage in itself holds a lot of meaning. Many people will consider this passage and immediately discuss it as related to corporal punishment—'spare the rod, spoil the child." In actuality, training up a child in the way they should go encompasses much more than corporal punishment. This passage refers to the love of a child, the structure of the home, raising and training them to walk with the Lord, and most importantly the grooming of the child to walk in the Spirit and produce the fruit of the Spirit. Train up a child in the way that they should go so when they get older, they will not depart from the foundation that we have already set for them.

In addition to training up the child in the way they should go, we have to be mindful of their tender spirit. This is especially true of our young children who are now witnessing and experiencing terrorist attacks and crime on a regular basis. There was a time in which the occurrence of terrorist attacks was rare. However, in this modern time, our children are exposed to trauma frequently. It was just in December of 2012 that we had the unfortunate event of the Connecticut shooting where small school-aged children were shot and killed. Not even six months later was the Boston marathon attack. Someone set a bomb at this historical race to create fear in the hearts and minds of the people. Such events are not only creating fear, but also creating a fear mentality. Our young people not only represent new fads, wild hair, and crazy music, but in fact, they are the next generation. Satan realizes this more than we do; children represent a new generation and the future of the church. Satan desires to smear this new generation with havoc by depositing fear into their spirit. Fear is not only a matter of being afraid, but it creates desperation. Now imagine the state of America and the church if the future generation is paralyzed with fear. They will be so desperate to be safe that they will do anything and possibly bow to anyone. What types of compromises might they make with other nations—and even Satan himself?

How should we combat fear in our children? We have to take time to sit down, talk, and minister to our children about the love of God. We cannot promise them that turmoil and travesty will never happen again, because it will. The Bible speaks of chaos in the end times. However, it is very important that we explain the truth of the end times to our children, help them stand on the promises of God, and let them know that everything is going to be all right. We have to explain to them the promise of heaven; even if we lose our life, we will find it again. *"Let not your hearts be troubled. Ye believe in God, believe also in me. In my father's house are many mansions: if it were not so, I would have told you. I go to prepare a place for you. And if I go to prepare a place for you, I will come again, and receive you unto myself; that where I am, there ye may be also"* (John 14:1-3).

Chapter XIV

TO THE ABUSER

I t is a vast misconception that the abuser is having fun, delighted, and enjoying his life and role as the abuser. In actuality, there is something seriously damaged in the heart and psyche of the abuser. They very well may hate themselves. That is, there is a level of anger, hurt, and scorn for their very being and conscious, that we may never understand. The phrase 'emotional problems or mental illness' is an understatement for abusers. This idea is expanded to groups because if we consider terrorist groups, their motivating force is hatred and fear. There is a deep, intense fear that the opposing party will overpower them. If we consider abusers, they somehow consider themselves inadequate and often see the opposing party as better, smarter, and more powerful than they are. They must take extreme measures to create fear and thus destroy the spirit of their opposition. The abuser is suffering with thoughts of inadequacy and feeling less worthy than everyone in his environment.

Unfortunately, many of us will read the above information and likely begin to feel sorry for our 'suffering' abuser. We will become empathic and may even attempt to reach out into the depths of our abuser's heart to try to heal his pain. This is an uphill battle; it will only place our spirit in danger of further emotional abuse. By now we should realize, he does not want our love or our help. In spite of the vast amount of pain the abuser is suffering, we cannot forget that his decision to be an abuser is a personal choice and is intentional.

Nevertheless, the abuser is suffering. His suffering may not look like our suffering, but still indicates a malfunction in his spirit. He is unable to walk in the Spirit and produce the fruit of the Spirit. The fact is, only God can effectively heal the abuser's pain and suffering, and only God can renew his mind and spirit.

If anyone was an abuser, it was the Apostle Paul, formerly known as Saul of Tarsus. His story and testimony can be read in the book of Acts (KJV). Saul, based on his actions and behaviors at the time, could have been rightly labeled a terrorist. He wanted to exert his power so much over the believers that he was willing to do anything. Saul took extreme measures; he approached the high court in an effort to gain authority and commission from the chief priests to torture and kill believers. Saul was fearful that the believers would somehow overpower the cities, so he went about torturing, scattering, and killing innocent people of God.

It was one day while on a trip to Damascus to torture and slaughter the Christians that an angel appeared to

Saul. *"And as he journeyed, he came near Damascus: and suddenly there shined round about him a light from heaven: And he fell to the earth, and heard a voice saying unto him, Saul, Saul, why persecutest thou me? And he said, Who art thou, Lord? And the Lord said, I am Jesus whom thou persecutes"* (Acts 9:3-5). Saul, an abuser, was convicted in his spirit. Saul was converted and from thenceforward became known as the Apostle Paul. The same Apostle Paul wrote most of the Bible. From that moment, Paul made the choice to live for God. He became a preacher and teacher of the Gospel; he established churches, and lived a consecrated life, holy and acceptable unto God, which he believed it was his reasonable service.

If you are an abuser, you can make a change today. The fact is *"God sent not his son into the world to condemn the world, but that the world through Him might be saved"* (John 3:17). We do not know what happened in your past to cause you to carry such hatred towards yourself to the point you are hurting and abusing others. However, one thing is certain; by reading this book, you know the truth and are accountable for your actions. Seek help now. Do not continue to sulk in self-pity with your 'woe is me' mind frame. "I only do this because it was done to me." Getting help and changing your life is not only going to benefit you, but your children, their children, and future generations.

In reviewing the story of Tamar, we saw the events that occurred before the abuse, the mentality of the abuser and victim, the emotional damage that was created, and the overall sin involved. The effects of evil are sin and the effects of sin are evil. Have you heard of generational curses? The abuse in your life will continue into the next generation. Unless the Holy Spirit intervenes, it will become a vicious cycle; sin, evil, sin, evil. Unless you stop now and start to walk in the Spirit, the abuse that happened to you will continue to have power in your life.

If you have admitted to yourself that you are an abuser, perhaps you now feel lost and out of control. This means the Holy Spirit is convicting you. There is hope for you. The savior is standing with His arms wide open. It is very important for you to understand that all is not lost. If you think you cannot change, please believe that thought is only Satan's trap and desire to keep you walking in the lust of the flesh. Christ says, *"I have not come to call the righteous, but sinners to repentance"* *(Luke 5:32).* This means God is calling you; despite all that you have done, God loves you. It is time for you to get help, repent, change, and live as the person God has called and ordained you to be. If you want to make a change to day, here is your opportunity to say the sinner's prayer.

Heavenly Father in the name of Jesus, I thank you for the ability to come before your throne knowing that you hear me. Lord, you know all things and you see all things. I cannot hide anything from you. I am a sinner. Up until this time, I have hurt myself and people around me. At this time, I choose to surrender my life to you. I ask you to forgive me for all of my sins. I ask you to make me clean. God, I believe that you sent your son Jesus to die on the cross for my sins. I now accept your grace and repent of my sins. I confess with my mouth and I believe in my heart that you have raised your son Jesus from the dead. I accept you as my Lord and Savior. I believe I am now saved. Father, I accept the power of your Holy Spirit to change me. I ask that you help me to walk in your ways and dedicate my life to you. I believe all these things in your son Jesus name. Thank you for my new life in you. Amen.

If you said the prayer and believed it in your heart, you are now saved. Now it is time for you to go and find a Bible believing church. Reading this book was just the beginning. I believe the information in this book has activated change in your heart. God has started a good work in you and He will perform it. God is a man of his word; He will do just what he said.

Chapter XV

FOR HIS GLORY

T he name 'Tamar' means palm tree. The palm tree is one of the tallest and most flexible trees in the world. When a storm or strong wind blows, a palm tree will bend—sometimes all the way over, but it will not break. *"We are troubled on every side, yet not distressed; we are perplexed, but not in despair; Persecuted, but not forsaken; cast down, but not destroyed"* (2 Cor. 4:8-9). As well, the palm tree bears one of the sweetest fruit— the date. When considering Tamar's story, she never recovered from her abuse. Her spirit was broken and she remained desolate; she was never able to bear fruit.

"I am Tamar" means that we have an awesome opportunity to stand tall like a palm tree and live out the joyous life Tamar never experienced. Unlike Tamar, we all have the incredible opportunity to be a living testimony. We do not have to remain desolate. God wants us to be healed and bear fruit. *"But the fruit of the Spirit is love, joy, peace, longsuffering, gentleness, goodness, faith, meekness, and temperance"* (Gal. 5:22-23).

137

Everything that we have been through has been for a purpose. *"And we know that all things work together for the good of them who love God and are called according to his purpose"* (Rom. 8:28). God wants to get the glory out of our life.

In 2007, I married a man whom I loved dearly. He was my first boyfriend and first sexual partner. When my marriage ended in 2011, I felt as if a diesel truck had hit me. I felt as if I had been cheated out of love and I questioned God about it. I also felt guilty that I had divorced and my children would not experience having both parents under the same roof as I did. I prayed vigorously for God to save my marriage, but it ended anyway. The fact is God was not obligated to keep a relationship together that He did not put together in the first place.

Immediately after our separation and throughout the divorce, I could recall everything my husband had done to me. I remembered all the hurt and pain. My memories were very vivid—as if I was reliving them. In my mind, our marital problems were his fault entirely and I had no problem pointing my finger at him. I wanted him to suffer for everything he did to me. I soon became even angrier as I saw him almost immediately moving forward in his life. One night, I saw him at church and I thought, "He has the nerve to be here. He is not even saved."

As God began to deal with me, He showed me that I was not without sin. *"He who is without sin among you, let him cast a stone"* (John 8:7). I had been so desperate to be in a relationship and be married that I fell out of the will of God. That is, I placed my new relationship in front of God. Before I knew it, I had started to follow the lust of my flesh. I was no longer spending time with the Lord in prayer and meditation. I stopped being faithful to my church and lost focus on God's plan for my life.

When the situation became worse in my marriage, instead of seeking God, I began fighting, fussing, and cursing. The problems in my marriage had changed me from the humorous, compassionate, woman of worship that I was, into someone who was bitter, resentful, and full of hatred; I had lost my identity. If I had listened to the voice of God, the counsel of my pastor, and my family, I would not have been in that situation. The truth is I had abandoned my first love—God. God is a jealous God. He wanted all of me and would not tolerate to be second, especially when He had such a calling on my life. The fact is, God used my pain and heartache to bring me back to Him. God also reminded me that it is not His desire that anyone should perish and I should be glad to know that my ex-husband is in church. *"The Lord is not slack concerning his promise, as some men count slackness; but is longsuffering to us-ward, not willing that any should perish, but that all should come to repentance"* (2 Pet. 3:9).

Today, I feel God's love more than I ever did before. A little while after my ex-husband left, he said to me, "After all of this is over, you are going to have a powerful testimony." Today, as I write the last few sentences of this book, his words ring loudly in my ears. I know that everything I suffered was for God's glory. I am living in expectation of what God has for me. When I remarry, it will not be for me, it will be for Him. In other words, my marriage will not be for my own benefit, but it will be for God's glory. I am determined that God will get the glory out of my marriage, children, and career; I surrender every aspect of my life over to Him. I am Tamar, but I am healed. To God be the glory for the things He has done.

BIBLIOGRAPHY

Brady, L. (2012). Personal communication on 'universal loss theory.' Phoenix, AZ.

Brewer, A. (2012). *Fighting All Hell for Your Marriage, Your man, and Your Babies*. Indianapolis, IN: IBJ Book Publishing.

Clinton, T. & Hawkins, R. (2011). *The Popular Encyclopedia of Christian Counseling*. Eugene, Oregon: Harvest House Publishers.

Kikuyu, T. (2013, January 5). The living more abundantly talk radio show [Radio Broadcast]. Phoenix, AZ: El Shaddai Radio.

Scott, T. (2009, January). "Trusting God." Sermon presented at Harvest Celebration Evangelistic Church of God in Christ, Jackson, MS.

Yerkes, M. (2007). FAQs about emotional abuse. *Focus on the Family*. Retrieved January 1, 2013, from http://www.focusonthefamily.com/lifechallenges/ abuse_and_addiction/understanding_emotional_ abuse/faqs_about_emotional_abuse.aspx.

CPSIA information can be obtained
at www.ICGtesting.com
Printed in the USA
LVOW01s1354060217
523351LV00012B/173/P